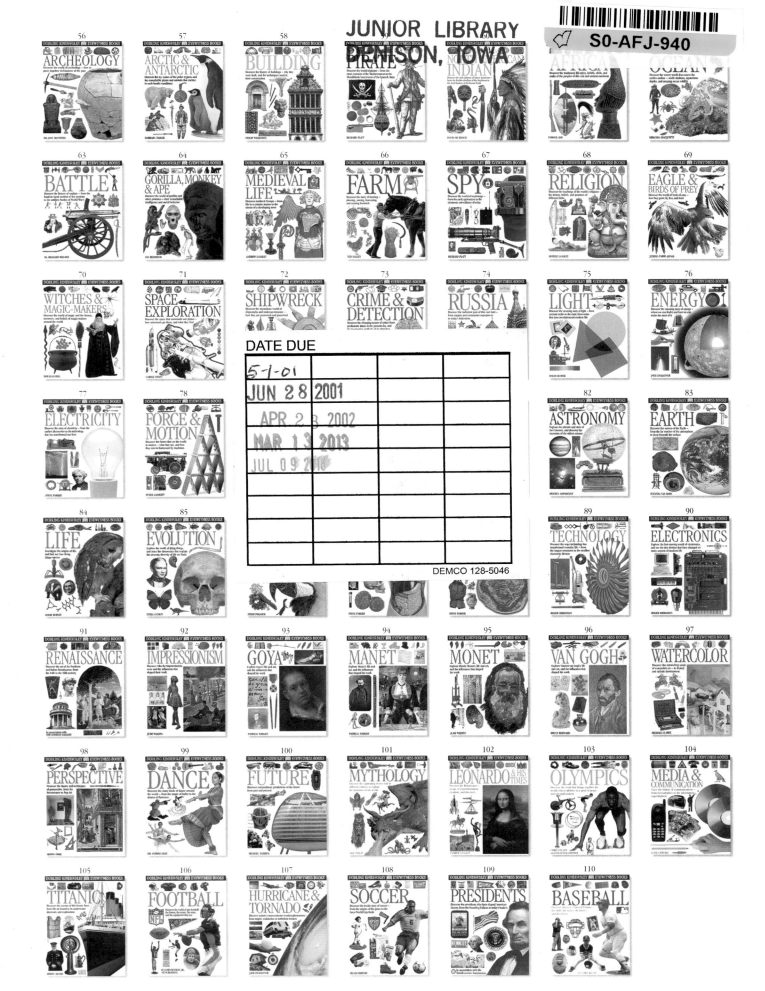

DORLING KINDERSLEY 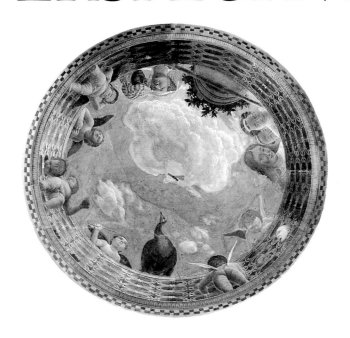 EYEWITNESS BOOKS

PERSPECTIVE

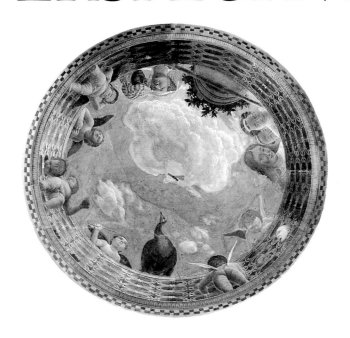

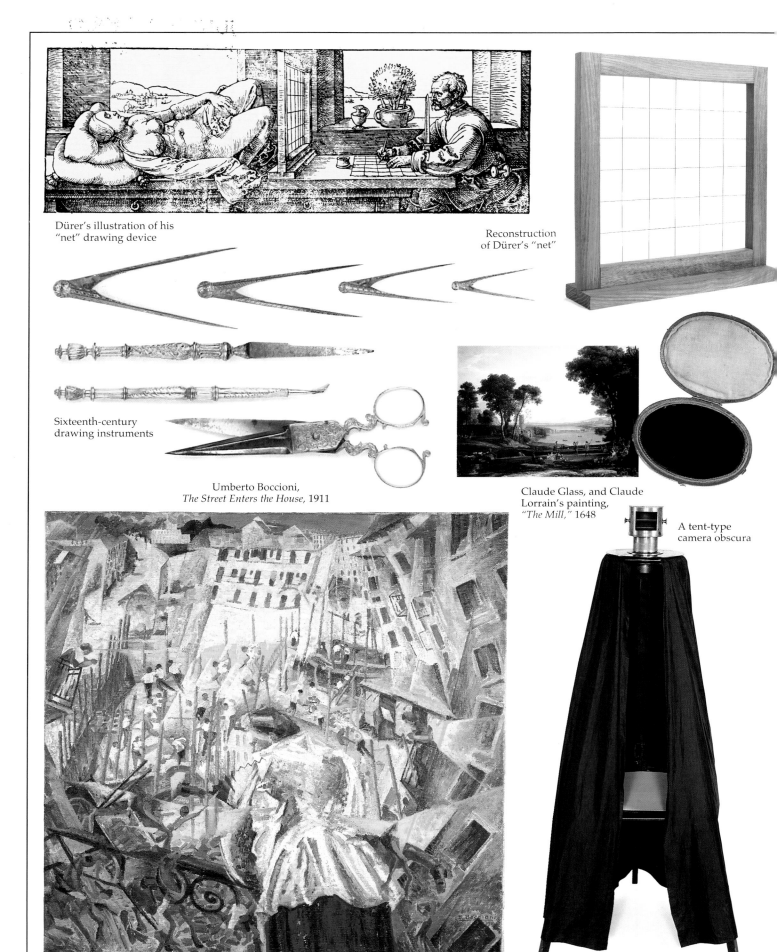

Dürer's illustration of his
"net" drawing device

Reconstruction
of Dürer's "net"

Sixteenth-century
drawing instruments

Umberto Boccioni,
The Street Enters the House, 1911

Claude Glass, and Claude
Lorrain's painting,
"The Mill," 1648

A tent-type
camera obscura

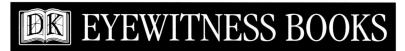

EYEWITNESS BOOKS

PERSPECTIVE

ALISON COLE

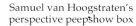

Samuel van Hoogstraten's
perspective peepshow box

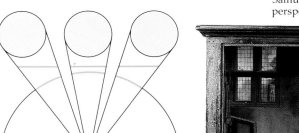

Leonardo's theory of
Curvilinear Perspective

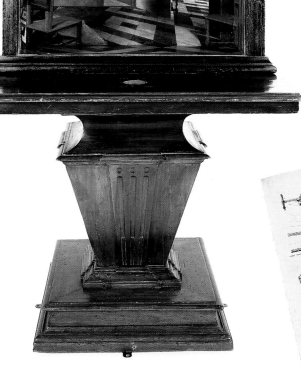

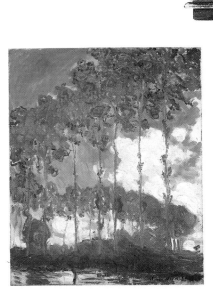

Claude Monet, *Poplars
on the Epte*, 1891

Encyclopedia
illustrations of specialist
drawing instruments

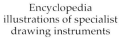

Dorling Kindersley

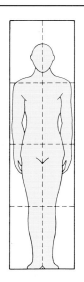

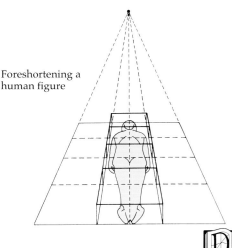

Foreshortening a
human figure

Early medieval
crucifix

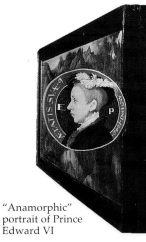

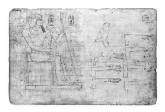

Egyptian drawing

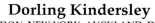

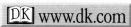

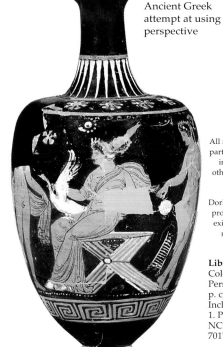

Ancient Greek
attempt at using
perspective

Dorling Kindersley

LONDON, NEW YORK, AUCKLAND, DELHI,
JOHANNESBURG, MUNICH, PARIS and SYDNEY

For a full catalog, visit

DK www.dk.com

Project editor Ann Kay
Project and series art editor Toni Rann
Editorial and visual researcher Julia Harris-Voss
Design assistant Claire Pegrum
Technical consultant Dr Philip Steadman
Managing editor Sean Moore
Managing art editor Tina Vaughan
US editor Laaren Brown
DTP manager Joanna Figg-Latham
DTP designer Doug Miller
Production controller Meryl Silbert
Consultants David Bomford, Jill Dunkerton, Dr Erika
Langmuir, Dr Nicholas Penny, National Gallery, London

This Eyewitness ® Book has been conceived by
Dorling Kindersley Limited and Editions Gallimard

© 1992 Dorling Kindersley Limited
This edition © 2000 Dorling Kindersley Limited
First American edition, 1992
Published in the United States by
Dorling Kindersley Publishing, Inc.
95 Madison Avenue
New York, NY 10016
2 4 6 8 10 9 7 5 3 1

Library of Congress Cataloging-in-Publication Data
Cole, Alison.
Perspective / written by Alison Cole.
p. cm. — (Eyewitness Books)
Includes index.
1. Perspective. I. Title. II. Series.
NC750.S49 2000
701'. 82—dc20
92-7059
CIP
ISBN 0-7894-6178-1 (pb)   ISBN 0-7894-5585-4 (hc)

Color reproduction by Colourscan, Singapore
Printed in China by Toppan Printing Co. (Shenzhen) Ltd.

Renaissance
dividers

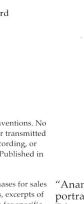

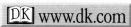

"Anamorphic"
portrait of Prince
Edward VI

Contents

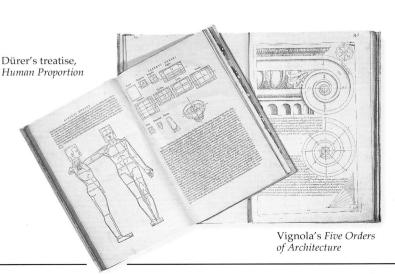

Dürer's treatise,
Human Proportion

Vignola's *Five Orders
of Architecture*

What is perspective?

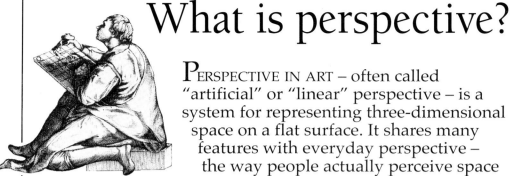

PERSPECTIVE IN ART – often called "artificial" or "linear" perspective – is a system for representing three-dimensional space on a flat surface. It shares many features with everyday perspective – the way people actually perceive space and objects in it. However, because linear perspective is based on the fixed viewpoint of one eye, and is worked out mathematically, it can only approximate the complex way the eyes actually function. As a science, perspective is closely related to optics (the study of the laws of sight) – a discipline that flourished in Ancient Greece and Rome and during the Middle Ages. But, as a pictorial system, it was only fully developed in the early 15th century, in the pioneering experiments of Filippo Brunelleschi and Leon Battista Alberti (pp. 12–13). Alberti compared the picture surface to "... an open window through which the subject painted is to be seen."

AIDS TO ACCURACY
For centuries, artists have used a range of devices to gain perspectival accuracy.

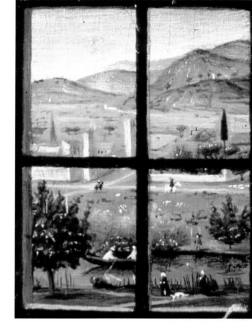

ST. JEROME IN HIS STUDY *right, and detail above*
Antonello da Messina; c.1475; 18 x 14¼ in
(46 x 36 cm); oil on lime wood
This is a perfect illustration of the early Renaissance idea of a picture as a view through a window. It includes an illusionistic arched stone surround and a window ledge that gives way to the intricate checkerboard floor of the saint's orderly study. The painting even includes a squared window in the background (above), through which a vivid distant landscape can be seen.

THE ROLE OF THE EYE
Perspective theory is based on the way a single eye perceives an object. Light reflects from any one surface and travels in straight rays to the eye. "Extreme" rays define the boundaries (size and shape) of the surface; "median" rays convey color and tone; and a single "centric" ray reflects at right angles from the point on which the eye is focused (Diagram 1). The picture "plane" (surface) is like a glass sheet that intercepts these rays (Diagram 2). Where the rays "pass through" this plane, a scale image of the object can be plotted.

Diagram 1
Surface (plane) of actual object
90°

Diagram 2
Picture plane
Actual object
Scale image

Red = centric ray
Blue = median rays
Black = extreme rays

Central meeting, or "vanishing" point

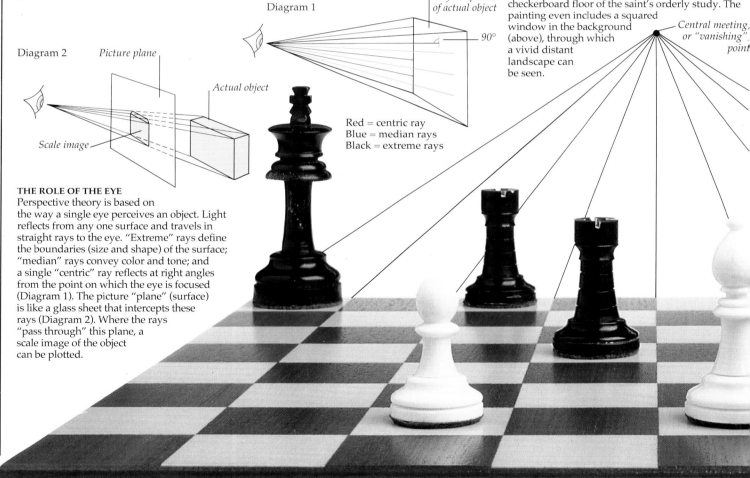

A CLOSE MEETING *right*
In this detail of the Hogarth print
shown below, the old woman
appears to be lighting the pipe
of the traveler in the distance!

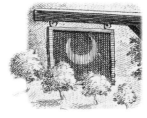

OUT OF PLACE
left
The faraway trees overlap a
giant inn sign, which somehow
manages to project from the
public house in the foreground

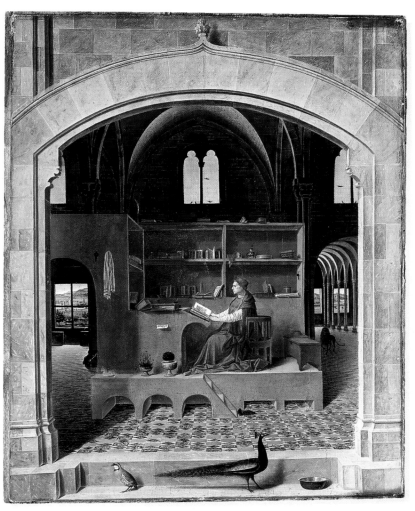

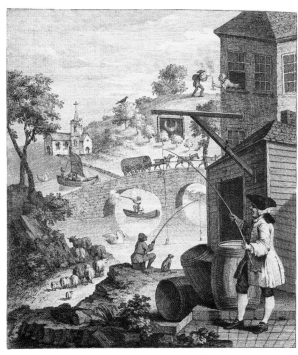

OVERTURNING CONVENTIONS *above*
William Hogarth's witty print *Perspectival Absurdities*
(1754) – used as the frontispiece of a perspective
handbook – shows illogicalities due entirely to
deliberate mistakes in perspective and lighting. We
read it as a satire, rather than as a nonsensical image,
because the ability to interpret perspective clues has
become part of the way we look at pictures. A convincing perspective image (such as *St. Jerome*, above left) is
based on what we expect a realistic picture to look like.
Without the convention of perspective, we would not
make many basic assumptions – such as expecting
images to diminish in size as they recede.

*Because this king is
closer to the eye, it
appears much larger
than the king on the
other side of
the board*

LITTLE OR LARGE?
The sheep in this comic procession
become larger as they
disappear
from view.

THE SQUARED PAVEMENT PRINCIPLE
In many early Renaissance paintings, such as *St. Jerome* (top), a checkerboard
floor stretching away behind the picture surface provides the linear framework
for the painting's perspective construction. The basic visual rules of such
a framework can be seen in this chessboard. First, all the receding
parallel lines (which actually run at right angles to the front edge
of the board), appear to converge toward a central vanishing
(meeting) point as they get farther away. Second, all the
lines running parallel to the front edge of the board
remain parallel, although the spaces between
them (which are actually equal) look smaller
the farther away they appear. This effect
is known as "foreshortening." Third,
pieces that are farther away from the
eye appear smaller than those that are
closer: an effect called "diminution."

Early approaches

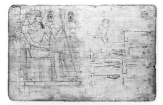

PERSPECTIVE CONVENTIONS have played such a central role in Western art, from the 15th century onward, that it is easy to regard earlier art as primitive. We are used to viewing images as mirrors of the world around us, but art has not always been based on the desire to paint what we see. The Ancient Egyptians, who had a rich artistic tradition, showed little interest in creating realistic illusions of space and depth. Their art used a rigid language of religious and social symbols. In contrast, the Ancient Greeks began to replace the pictorial language that they had been using with images based on how they actually saw. The Romans pursued this, creating naturalistic landscapes and elaborate architectural perspectives. With the collapse of the Roman Empire, these skills were rejected by the Byzantines, who returned to an art of divine symbols and order. It was only in the 13th and 14th centuries, with a renewed interest in the art of Ancient Rome, that the idea of art as a "mirror" resurfaced.

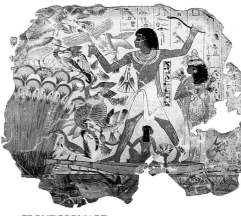

FRONT FORWARD
In Ancient Egyptian art, only the front planes of objects are shown. Figures are assembled from separate views: profiles for faces, arms, and legs; front views for eyes and chests. Depth is often suggested by overlapping forms, although here the inside of the boat is also shown.

The Virgin and Child with Saints
DUCCIO DI BUONINSEGNA
c.1315; center panel: 24 x 15¼ in (61.5 x 39 cm); egg tempera on poplar

Duccio's solemn altarpiece harks back to the sacred images of Byzantine art. The gold background lends majesty and an internal light; it also denies any sense of depth, allowing the holy participants to inhabit an entirely spiritual space. The figures themselves, however, have been modeled in light and shade, giving them a powerful physical presence.

Left panel:
St. Dominic

Right panel:
St. Aurea

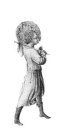

In order to tell the story clearly, St. John is the same size in the middle distance and foreground

ST. JOHN THE BAPTIST RETIRING TO THE DESERT
Giovanni di Paolo; c.1454; 12¼ x 15¼ in (31 x 39 cm); tempera on poplar
This small panel is unusual, as it combines the early Renaissance fascination with new perspective techniques and the old medieval convention of combining two episodes of a story in one scene. St. John is thus shown twice: once leaving the town, and again heading toward the desert. The latter is the composition's true subject, and so the intricate geometric patchwork of vineyards is shown from the bird's-eye view of the saint as he climbs the hill.

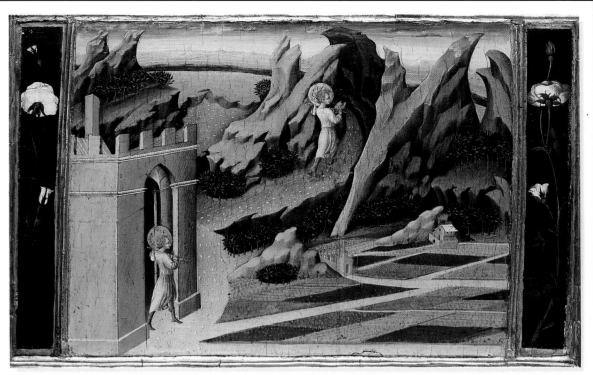

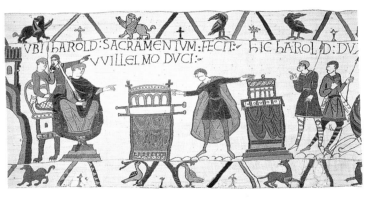

MEDIEVAL STORYTELLING
In the famous Bayeux Tapestry (c.1080), the figures are highly stylized, and there is little attempt at creating an illusion of space. For example, the sedan chair (the left-hand vacant chair) is flattened out into the foreground plane. However, the overlapping forms, and the fact that most figures are shown in three-quarter view, demonstrate an attempt at suggesting pictorial depth. The tapestry's makers suggested the solidity of forms through a technique called "couching," in which woolen threads are laid in parallel lines and then stitched to create solid blocks that stand out from the surface.

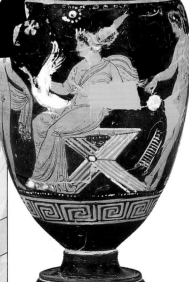

THREE-DIMENSIONAL FURNITURE
Paintings on Ancient Greek vases exhibit an early form of perspective that was based on observation rather than on mathematical rules. By the 4th century B.C., three-dimensional objects were often shown. This vase depicts the goddess Aphrodite sitting on a highly convincing stool; the diagram below shows how its far legs are foreshortened, so that they appear on a plane further back than the front ones. However, the seat is painted in the front plane only, making the illusion of depth incomplete.

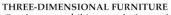

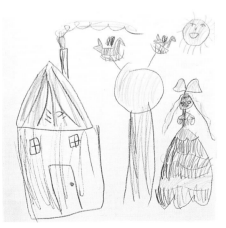

CHILD'S-EYE VIEW
Children's drawings suggest that it is innate in human nature to draw without depth – flattening everything into the foreground plane. This type of art is described as "conceptual" – based on an idea or notion about something, rather than on the way it is actually perceived. The size of objects is also affected: those that are most important to the child are usually shown the largest.

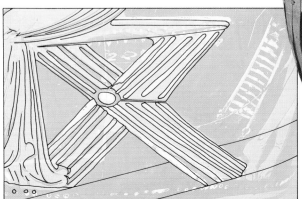

Defining space

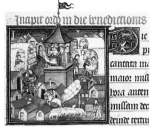

Bᴇꜰᴏʀᴇ ᴛʜᴇ ʀᴇɴᴀɪꜱꜱᴀɴᴄᴇ "invention" of linear perspective, artists had discovered many of the rules for themselves; all they lacked was the mathematical foundation that would have given their perspectives a logic and consistency. The Ancient Romans had developed a highly rational system, based on optical rules, which was used to great effect by theatrical set designers of the time. In the 13th and 14th centuries, Italian artists devised more intuitive schemes, based on a combination of natural observation and simple measurement. In Northern Europe, on the other hand, painters concentrated on the method of judging by eye. Through a minute study of nature, color, and light, they solved many of the problems that their Italian counterparts were still confronting.

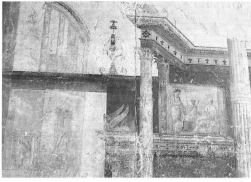

ANCIENT DECEPTION
According to the classical writer Vitruvius, the Romans used an optical system for constructing three-dimensional space, with a fixed central point to which all lines "should naturally correspond, with due regard to the point of sight and the extension of the visual rays, so that by this deception a faithful representation of the buildings might be given ..." In this Ancient Roman mural, the architecture looks so three-dimensional that it appears to project beyond the wall surface.

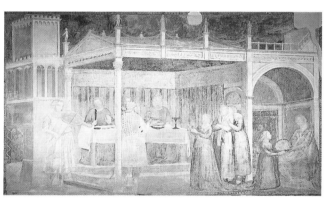

HEROD'S FEAST
Giotto di Bondone; c.1320s; fresco
Giotto (c.1267–1337) introduced a new realism by creating convincing spatial environments. Here, he angles the building, removing front and side walls to reveal its cubic interior. Around 1400, the theorist Cennino Cennini devised a crude rule based on Giotto's procedure: "The moldings at the base of the building must slant upward in the opposite direction to the upper moldings which slant downward."

The Presentation in the Temple
AMBROGIO LORENZETTI
1342; 8 ft 5 in x 5 ft 6 in (2.57 x 1.68 m); tempera on wood
In this panel, the perspective image has almost arrived. There is a far greater impression of depth than in Giotto, achieved partly by the diminishing size of the floor tiles. The receding lines of the floor converge toward a single focus (vanishing point), although the other receding diagonals converge toward points higher up in the picture.

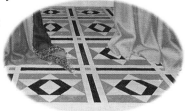

Squared floors are an effective way of demonstrating recession

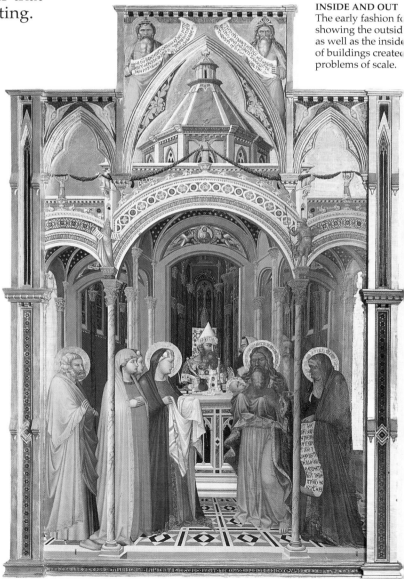

INSIDE AND OUT
The early fashion for showing the outside as well as the inside of buildings created problems of scale.

"The Arnolfini Marriage"

JAN VAN EYCK *1434*

32¼ x 23½ in (82 x 60 cm); oil on oak

Netherlandish master van Eyck (d.1441) created highly convincing interiors and landscapes through empirical means – that is, by relying on his own observations rather than on theoretical rules. He also studied everything so closely that his eye has been described as "both a telescope and a microscope." In this painting, an intimate interior is created by the sloping lines of the boarded floor and beamed ceiling, the relative size of objects, and the sensitive use of light.

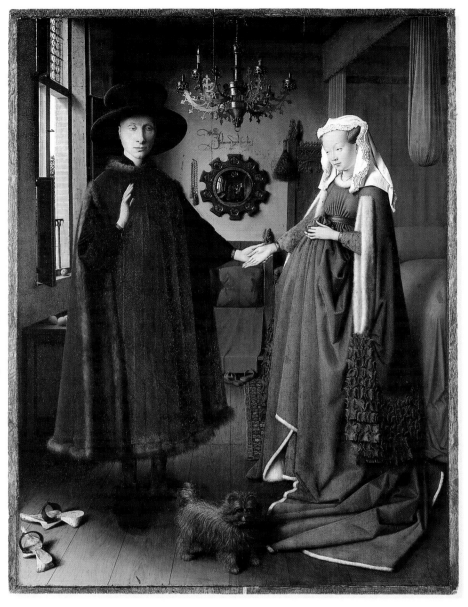

The deep reflection reveals two extra figures

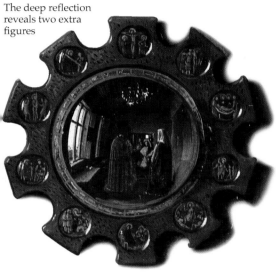

MIRROR IMAGE

A convex mirror, like that in the *Arnolfini* picture, may have been used by van Eyck as a compositional aid. Some artists in the north are known to have copied the concentrated perspective images seen in convex mirrors as a means of creating forceful effects of light, space, and depth. The exaggerated curves of the reflection would have been reduced in the final work.

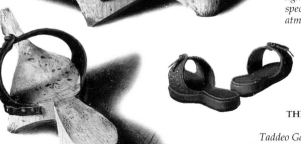

The strong shadows emphasize the role of light in creating a specific spatial atmosphere

COMPARATIVE SIZES

The two pairs of shoes lying on the floor, one in the background and one in the foreground, show that clues of size are vital to the overall impression of space and distance.

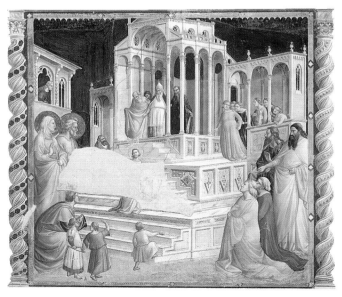

THE PRESENTATION OF THE VIRGIN

Taddeo Gaddi; after 1328; fresco
Giotto's pupil Taddeo Gaddi (d.1366) adopted the tilted architecture construction used by his master. In *The Presentation of the Virgin*, he took this approach to new extremes, combining it with a wealth of naturalistic detail. The effect is impressive, but the composition fails to tell the story clearly, and clear story-telling was to be an important part of the Renaissance perspective image.

The "invention" of perspective

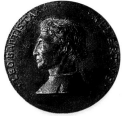

Bronze Italian medal, 1440s, showing Alberti

THE PICTORIAL SYSTEM of linear perspective was developed during the early 15th century, in the unique intellectual and artistic climate of Renaissance Florence.

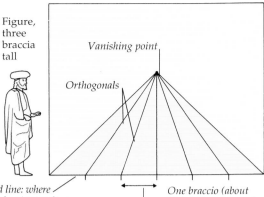

Figure, three braccia tall

Vanishing point

Orthogonals

Ground line: where base of the picture plane (p. 6) meets the ground

One braccio (about 23 in/57 cm), to scale

(p. 6)

ALBERTI'S METHOD, STAGE 1
Alberti based his system on the height of a human figure. He set this height at three "braccia" (about 6 ft / 1.8 m) – a "braccio" was a Renaissance unit of measurement. Having drawn a rectangular picture area, which Alberti imagined as an open window, he divided the ground line into scaled braccia. Next, he fixed the central vanishing point by drawing a vertical line three braccia high from the center of the ground line. This point is opposite the artist's viewpoint: Alberti imagined the artist and viewer to be the same height as a figure in the picture's foreground. He then drew lines – "orthogonals" – joining the ground line divisions to the vanishing point.

Two Florentines have been credited with its "invention" or rediscovery – the architect, artist, antiquarian, and man of letters Leon Battista Alberti (1404–1472), and the sculptor and architect Filippo Brunelleschi (1377–1446). Brunelleschi – who later achieved celebrity status with his great dome for Florence Cathedral – was the first to demonstrate the principles of linear perspective in his famous "peepshow" experiments (c.1413, below). But the underlying geometry seems to have been discovered by Alberti. His simple method (1435) enabled artists to create a deep, geometrically controlled space on a two-dimensional picture surface – and transformed the face of Western art.

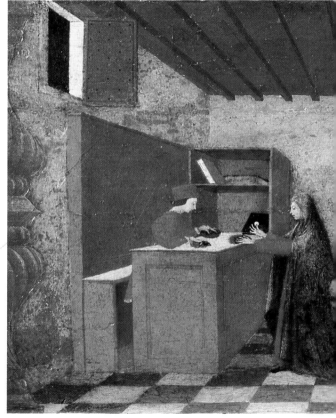

A burnished silver area on the panel reflected the real sky

BRUNELLESCHI'S "PEEPSHOW"
According to his biographer, Brunelleschi created the first true perspective panels (now lost). This artwork illustrates one of the panels – a view of Florence's Baptistry (the Church of San Giovanni), based on precise sightings taken from just inside the portal of the cathedral directly opposite. Brunelleschi demonstrated the panel's miraculous illusion of depth by boring a hole through it (at what was later called the vanishing point). The viewer held up the panel, pressing the hole to one eye (on the unpainted side), while holding up a mirror with the other hand so that the painting's reflection could be seen. A viewer standing in the Cathedral doorway (at the painting's viewpoint) could check the painted illusion against the real view.

From the Pollaiuolo brothers' *The Martyrdom of St. Sebastian* (1475)

THE ARROW AND THE EYE
As a simple way of explaining perspective in art, Renaissance theorists used the metaphor of the archer. Just as the archer closes one eye and aims the arrow at a fixed target, so the artist should imagine a straight line from the center of the eye to the composition's vanishing point.

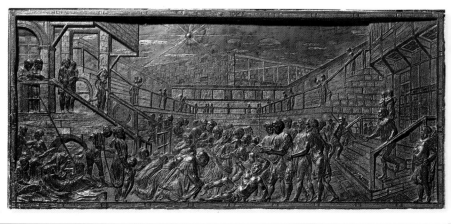

Alberti's system

Alberti's 1435 treatise *On Painting* set out the "best method" for constructing a picture's perspective. He imagined the picture surface as a plane cutting through a pyramid of visual rays (p. 6). These diagrams explain his system.

Viewpoint | Distance from viewer's eye to picture

Lines representing visual rays

SIDE VIEW — Picture plane (from edge) — Ground plane (p. 62)

STAGES 2 AND 3 – THE CHECKERBOARD PAVEMENT

For the next stages, Alberti drew a separate side view, showing the picture from the plane edge. He then divided the ground plane into braccia and marked the viewpoint to the left of the picture edge (having decided on the viewing distance and fixing the height at three braccia). Next, he drew visual rays from the viewpoint to the divisions on the ground plane. Where these rays cut through the picture edge (or plane) determined the positions of the horizontal lines ("transversals"). These were then added to the first-stage construction, creating a foreshortened checkered pavement. The "horizon" line is drawn through the vanishing point, parallel with the picture base. Alberti recommended drawing a diagonal line from the bottom left "tile" to the far right to check the construction's accuracy.

Vanishing point
Horizon line

Checkback line — **FRONT VIEW** — Transversals

POSITIONING OBJECTS IN SPACE

Having created a flat pavement of tiles stretching into the distance, Alberti could position objects using his one-braccio-to-a-tile scale. He drew the base (floor plan) of the object onto a squared grid and then transferred it onto the perspective grid. An object's height, at the front and the back, could then be plotted using measurements taken across the floor. This building has walls four braccia high (VP=Vanishing Point).

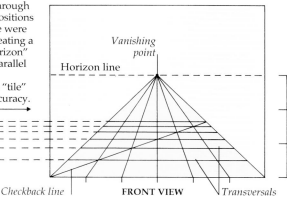

VP
4 braccia
4 braccia

The Selling of the Host

PAOLO UCCELLO *c.1468; one of six small narrative scenes shown in a row; dimensions of the whole row: 1 ft 4½ in x 11 ft 5¾ in (0.42 x 3.51 m); tempera on wood*

Although Alberti aimed to provide a formula that artists could adapt, this panel is an almost exact illustration of his system. The woman is three tiles high, measuring along the base of the picture (although, ideally, she should be placed more in the foreground), and the vanishing point is level with her head. The furniture shows that it was easier to foreshorten simple, regular shapes.

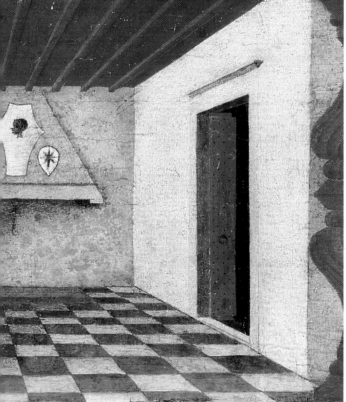

ST. ANTHONY HEALING THE YOUNG MAN'S FOOT *left and right Donatello; 1446–53; 22½ x 48½ in (57 x 123 cm); bronze panel, with gold and silver*
Alberti's one-vanishing-point system applies to all objects shown parallel to the picture plane. But when the bases of buildings, for instance, are at an angle to the picture plane, two vanishing points are used, both lying on the same horizon line (HL). In this panel by Donatello (1386–1466), the left-hand building and the right-hand stepped structure in the distance meet at a central vanishing point (black dot in center). The right-hand foreground building, however, leads to a second vanishing point (right-hand dot).

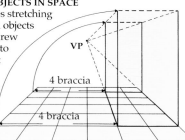

This "Ptolemaic" world map, 1486, uses a scale squared grid

MAPPING METHODS
Alberti's method may have been based partly on techniques used by ancient and medieval mapmakers and surveyors.

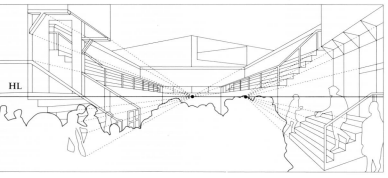

HL

From *The Martyrdom of St. Sebastian*

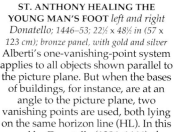

A "hole in the wall"

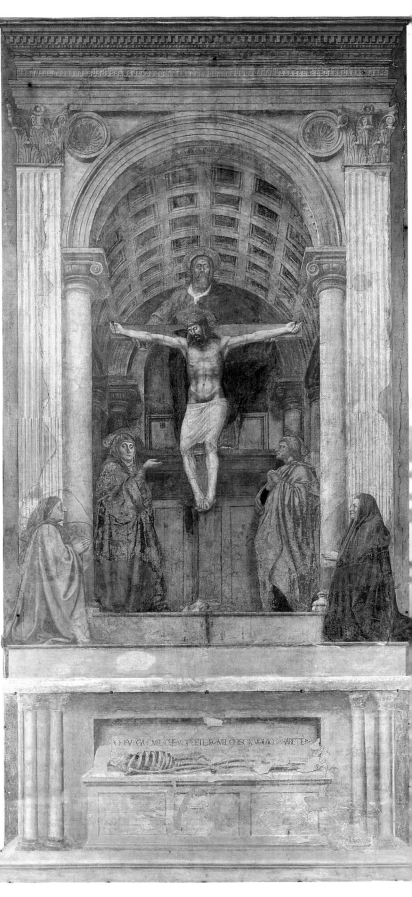

THE IMPORTANCE OF BRUNELLESCHI'S perspective experiments (p. 12) was first realized by the Florentine artist Masaccio (1401–28). His fresco of the *Trinity*, in the church of Santa Maria Novella, Florence, was one of the earliest paintings to use linear perspective rigorously. Its painted architectural framework is so carefully constructed that it could almost have been translated from an architectural plan – Brunelleschi may even have helped with its design. The convincing illusion of a two-tier chapel (which includes a tomb below) inspired Vasari, Masaccio's biographer, to comment that the wall on which the fresco was painted appeared "to have holes in it." Masaccio, however, veils the architectural detail in shadow, infusing the rigid geometry with the mystery of the Trinity (the threefold nature of God – the Father, Son, and Holy Ghost).

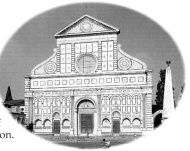

SANTA MARIA NOVELLA
The *Trinity* is one of the treasures of Sta. Maria Novella (right), whose facade was redesigned by Alberti (begun c.1456). Both facade and fresco illustrate the Renaissance ideals of harmony and proportion.

The Trinity

MASACCIO *c.1427; 21 ft 10½ in x 10 ft 5 in (6.7 x 3.2 m); fresco*
Masaccio's fresco compellingly recreates the "double chapel of Golgotha" (the place of Christ's Crucifixion) – a traditional medieval concept. The tomb of Adam (who represents man's sins) occupies the lower part of the fresco, while Christ's Crucifixion takes place in the space above. Together, these two elements symbolize man's redemption. The prayers of the two kneeling figures outside the chapel, aided by the Virgin and St. John the Evangelist, help the soul understand the mystery of the Trinity and reach salvation.

PERSPECTIVE REALISM
Lying on the painted tomb is Adam's skeleton, accompanied by the somber epitaph, "I was once that which you are, and what I am you will also be." Using the natural daylight that illuminated his fresco, as well as perspective illusionism, Masaccio gives it an astonishing sculptural reality. The perspective actually projects the skeleton into the real space of the church.

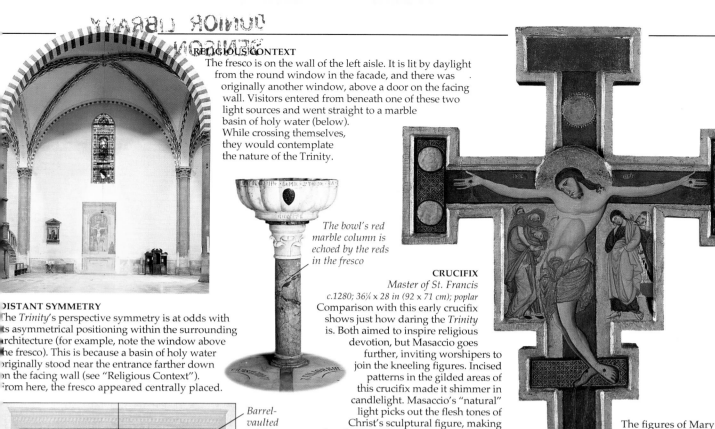

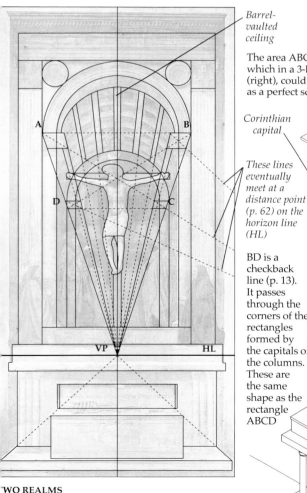

RELIGIOUS CONTEXT

The fresco is on the wall of the left aisle. It is lit by daylight from the round window in the facade, and there was originally another window, above a door on the facing wall. Visitors entered from beneath one of these two light sources and went straight to a marble basin of holy water (below). While crossing themselves, they would contemplate the nature of the Trinity.

The bowl's red marble column is echoed by the reds in the fresco

CRUCIFIX

Master of St. Francis
c.1280; 36¼ x 28 in (92 x 71 cm); poplar
Comparison with this early crucifix shows just how daring the *Trinity* is. Both aimed to inspire religious devotion, but Masaccio goes further, inviting worshipers to join the kneeling figures. Incised patterns in the gilded areas of this crucifix made it shimmer in candlelight. Masaccio's "natural" light picks out the flesh tones of Christ's sculptural figure, making him hover in front of the picture space.

DISTANT SYMMETRY

The *Trinity*'s perspective symmetry is at odds with its asymmetrical positioning within the surrounding architecture (for example, note the window above the fresco). This is because a basin of holy water originally stood near the entrance farther down on the facing wall (see "Religious Context"). From here, the fresco appeared centrally placed.

Barrel-vaulted ceiling

The area ABCD forms a rectangle, which in a 3-D reconstruction (right), could be interpreted as a perfect square

Corinthian capital

These lines eventually meet at a distance point (p. 62) on the horizon line (HL)

BD is a checkback line (p. 13). It passes through the corners of the rectangles formed by the capitals of the columns. These are the same shape as the rectangle ABCD

The figures of Mary (left) and St. John (right) are included in the side panels

The *Trinity* imitates the grand style of Classical architecture

Cornice
Frieze
Architrave

Ionic capital

Circular column

A "REAL" CHAPEL

Several attempts have been made to reconstruct Masaccio's chapel using precise measurements. This artwork gives an idea of what the architecture might have looked like if Masaccio had intended it to be read as an actual structure. If the coffers (the small panels on the ceiling) are assumed to be rectangles, then, following geometrical principles, the vault could be a perfect square space. The interior can then be explored, including the structure on which God stands – which some scholars suggest is Christ's tomb. It must be remembered, however, that the architecture is intended to convey a Christian mystery rather than clues to perspective.

Fluted pilaster

TWO REALMS

The perspective divides the space into two: the sacred space of the vaulted chapel, and the ordinary space that the kneeling figures and the skeleton share with the viewer. In both, orthogonals (p. 12) converge on a low vanishing point (VP) at eye level – Mary, John, and Christ are painted from below, but God – the all-present – is shown frontally.

Playful perspective

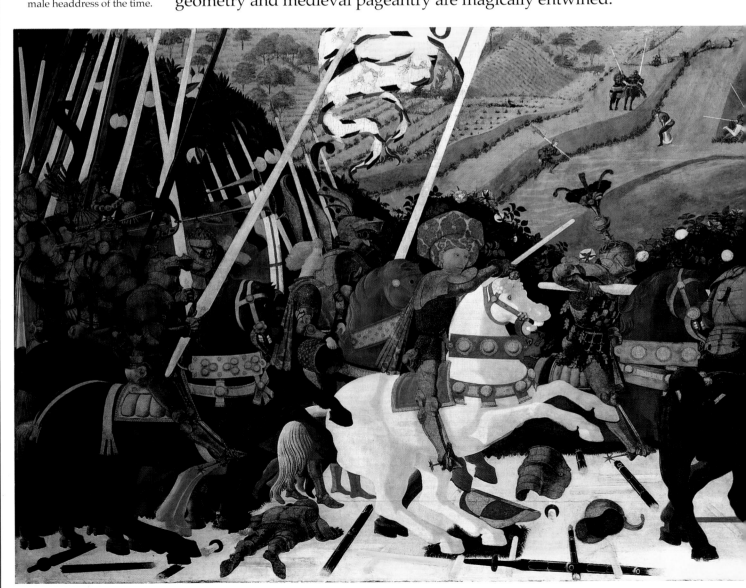

FOR PAOLO UCCELLO (c.1397–1475), perspective was a source of endless inspiration and delight. The Florentine painter wholeheartedly embraced this new discipline – excitedly exploring the geometry of animals, figures, and objects, as well as the mathematics of three-dimensional space. His biographer, Vasari, relates how, when Uccello's wife went to bed, he stayed up searching for vanishing points, declaring, "Oh, what a sweet thing this perspective is!" But Uccello was not simply a slave to perspective – he combined scientific probing with a love of medieval pattern and splendor. This can be seen in his exhilarating painting *The Battle of San Romano*, in which Renaissance geometry and medieval pageantry are magically entwined.

FACETS OF DESIGN
Uccello's meticulous drawing of a chalice is one of several studies showing how to solve perspective problems. The shape of the rim is based on a "mazzocchio": the wooden or wicker frame that supported a male headdress of the time.

The feet should actually be larger for the perspective to be totally consistent

FORESHORTENING
Uccello's striking use of foreshortening is shown by this soldier - from *The Battle of San Romano* – who has fallen down and died in perspective! He lies exactly on one of the diagonal lines that lead to the picture's compositional focus (p. 1

RSPECTIVE PUN
mmander Niccolò
Tolentino's hat
s been shown
a geometrical
ck shape – a
rspective pun
at would
ve delighted
naissance
ewers.

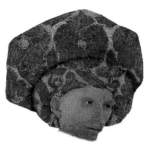

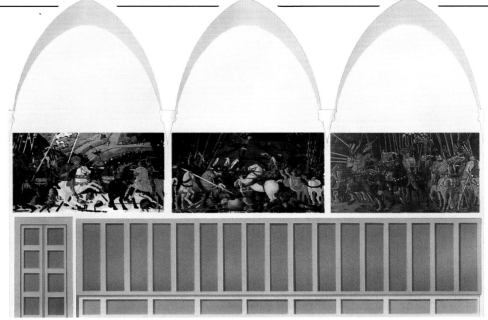

INTERIOR DECORATION

The Battle of San Romano is one of three Uccello paintings on the same subject. All three once hung together in the Medici Palace, Florence; this reconruction shows how they may have been arranged. The low viewpoint and consistent lighting of the intings suggest that they hung side by side, about 6½ ft (2 m) from the floor, with their landscapes orming a continuous link in the background. (The left-hand painting is now in the National Gallery, London; the center one in the Uffizi, Florence; the right-hand one in the Louvre, Paris.)

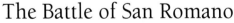

GUIDE LINES

To mark out the perspective framework of his paintings, Uccello used a metal stylus, possibly like the one at left, to score lines in the gesso (a preparatory layer of gypsum and glue). In the National Gallery *Battle*, the lances are placed along incised, ruled lines, which are still just visible.

THE FLOOD *right*
Paolo Uccello; c.1445; base: 16 ft 7 in (5.1 m); fresco
Uccello's dramatic use of perspective can be seen here – the viewer is pulled in by the force of the receding lines. The painting combines two biblical scenes: The Flood (left) and The Receding of the Flood (right). There are two vanishing points, and the lines to these cross in the distance – a way of providing a visual time lapse between the two episodes.

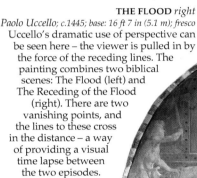

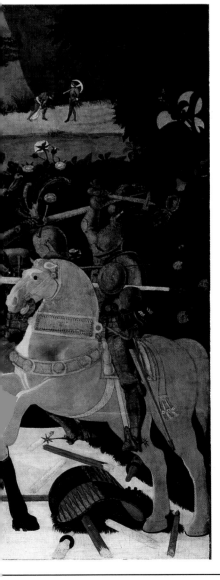

The Battle of San Romano

PAOLO UCCELLO *c.1450s; 5 ft 11½ in x 10 ft 6 in (1.82 x 3.20 m); egg tempera (possibly some oil) on poplar*
Uccello's *Battle of San Romano* (National Gallery, London) celebrates the Florentines' 1432 victory over the Sienese. The precise, mathematical construction of the foreground perspective, and the complex foreshortened poses of men and horses, are offset by decorative detail: the crisscross of lances, the soldiers' plumes, and the punched-gold harnesses of the prancing horses. The orange grove across the middle of the painting provides the perspective cutoff point, while the landscape beyond forms a "backdrop."

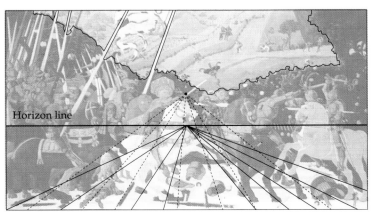

Horizon line

TWIN FOCUS

Broken lances converge on a vanishing point on the harness of Niccolò's horse, reflecting the low viewpoint of the work's original setting. Other diagonals – various lances, Niccolò's arm, the dead soldier, the leg of the horseman on Niccolò's right, and the hooves of the right-hand horse – form a compositional focus on Niccolò's hand, emphasizing him as the "hero" of the action.

Divine measurement

PIERO DELLA FRANCESCA (c.1415/20–1492), inspired by his belief in the perfect geometry underlying God's creation, devoted much of his life to the study of geometric solids and the mystical properties of numbers. In Piero's art, his mathematical genius can be seen in the harmony of the forms and the perspective consistency of his compositions. To him, a picture's construction was synonymous with measurement, and everything was defined by it – from inlaid pavements to the planes of a human face. In *The Flagellation*, the architectural proportions and dimensions have symbolic overtones, which, together with the use of light, reflect the divine order of things.

UNIVERSAL MATHEMATICS
This drawing of a mazzocchio (p. 16), from Piero's treatise on perspective, shows how the pure logic of mathematics governs even an ordinary item of headgear.

PERSPECTIVE PRACTICE
This illustration (right) shows painters how to foreshorten an octagonal floor pattern. It is one of the clear, detailed diagrams from Piero's important treatise, *De Prospectiva Pingendi (On the Perspective of Painting)*, written sometime before 1474. He intended the book to be used as a practical perspective aid, dealing with irregular shapes such as tilted human heads, as well as with architectural forms.

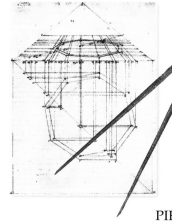

Detail of Christ from *The Flagellation*

ENGROSSING GEOMETRY
Piero's fascination with measurement, using instruments such as these dividers, led him to produce a substantial treatise entitled *De Quinque Corporibus Regolaribus (On the Five Regular Bodies)*. In this work, Piero reduced everything he saw to five regular geometric shapes.

THE MEASURE OF CHRIST
The Flagellation has been shown to be constructed around a single unit of measurement (1.85 in/4.69 cm). Another unit also plays a central role: 7 in (17.8 cm) – Christ's height in the painting. It has been suggested that Piero based this measurement, in a ratio of 1:10, on what was then thought to have been Christ's actual height – 5 ft 10 in (178 cm). This, in turn, was based on a famous relic – an ancient column measuring 5 ft 10 in. In Piero's time, this was in the Lateran Cloisters, Rome, and was believed to be the "measure" of the Son of God.

The Flagellation
PIERO DELLA FRANCESCA
c.1460; 23 x 32 in (58.5 x 81.5 cm); tempera on wood

This panel has eluded every attempt to unravel its full meaning. The most mysterious feature is the way the biblical scene of Christ's Flagellation is relegated to the background, while the foreground is dominated by three imposing and, as yet, unidentified figures. This mystery is emphasized by the distance (indicated with mathematical precision) between the scene of Christ's suffering and the three figures, and by the way in which they are separated by architectural columns.

ARCHITECTURE AND LIGHT *right*
The perspective of Piero's architectural setting is so logical and precise that scholars have been able to reconstruct the Flagellation room as if it were real architecture. Following the clues, the sharply foreshortened inlaid floor emerges in all the glory of its geometrical patterning. Light is manipulated with similar precision, to the extent that a mysterious secondary source has been discovered and located (see label "A"; the light is particularly noticeable on Christ's right side as we look at the painting). This light seems to have a supernatural significance – it is positioned directly in the line of Christ's gaze, and it has no possible natural source in the scene depicted.

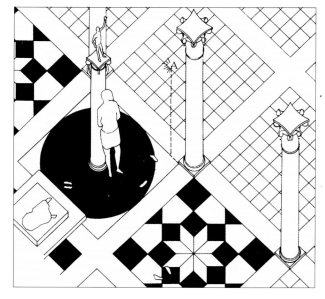

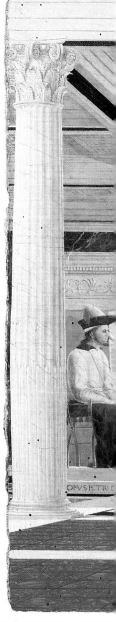

OPVS PETRI

FIGURE OF EIGHT

The eight figures in *The Flagellation* are intimately related to their architectural surroundings. Their number – eight – is deliberately echoed throughout the composition: in the large terra-cotta pavement squares, which are eight tiles deep and eight tiles wide; in the eight-pointed star on the pavement just behind and in front of Christ; and in the octagonal arrangement of the patterned floor tiles around the stars (p. 18). The piazza in which the foreground figures stand is eight units deep into the shade of the middle distance, and then another eight units deep into the light-flooded area in front of the far wall. In Christian symbolism, the number eight can allude to Christ's Resurrection. Was Piero making a reference to this in *The Flagellation*?

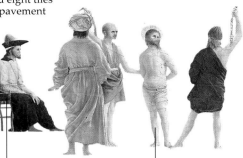

This figure is usually identified as Pilate

Christ being scourged by three soldiers

The three foreground figures may include the man who commissioned the painting – on the right in the brocade cloak

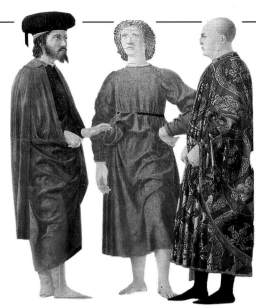

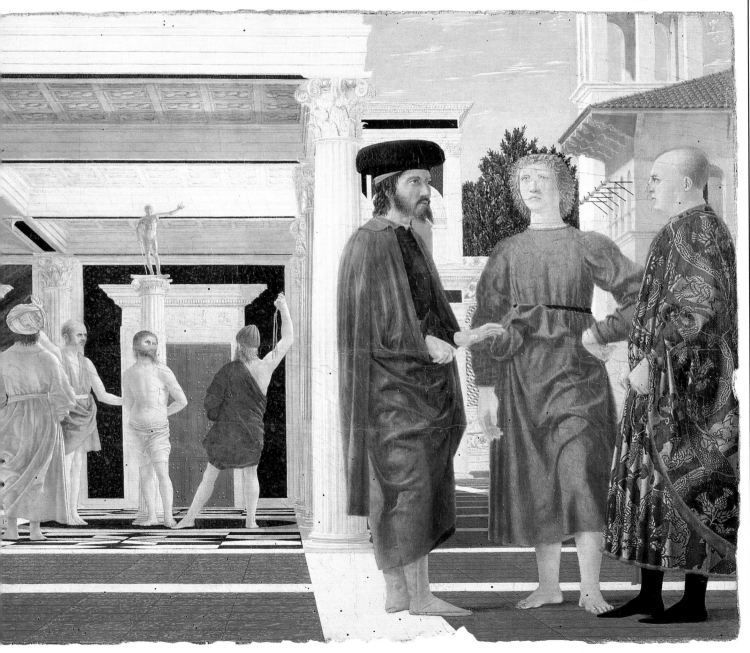

Eyewitness art

THE GREAT NORTHERN ITALIAN MASTER, Andrea Mantegna (1431–1506), was the first artist to explore fully the power of perspective over the spectator. Seizing on one of the principal aims of Alberti's system – that of deliberately guiding the viewer's eye through the narrative and controlling his or her response – Mantegna went one step further. With characteristic forcefulness and intensity, he propelled the viewer into the very heart of his drama. Spectators are therefore compelled to witness a scene, not from the comfort and distance of their own environment, but as if they were actually participating in the event. In some works, Mantegna's inventive manipulation of illusionistic effects makes the world of the picture break out of its boundaries and invade the viewer's space. The experience can be deeply moving, as in the *Dead Christ*, or delightfully entertaining, as in the humorous ceiling decoration of the "Painted Room" in the Gonzaga Palace, Mantua.

Mantegna's self-portrait bust adorns his tomb in Mantua

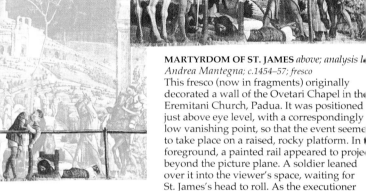

MARTYRDOM OF ST. JAMES *above; analysis l* *Andrea Mantegna; c.1454–57; fresco*
This fresco (now in fragments) originally decorated a wall of the Ovetari Chapel in the Eremitani Church, Padua. It was positioned just above eye level, with a correspondingly low vanishing point, so that the event seeme to take place on a raised, rocky platform. In foreground, a painted rail appeared to proje beyond the picture plane. A soldier leaned over it into the viewer's space, waiting for St. James's head to roll. As the executioner prepared to strike the guillotine, the viewer gazed into St. James's face. In that awful moment, the viewer became a bystander, waiting for the saint's head to fall into the chapel.

OCULUS, FROM "THE PAINTED ROOM" (*CAME PICTA***), IN THE GONZAGA PALACE, MANT** *Andrea Mantegna; 1465–74* *diameter: 8 ft 10 in (2.69 m); fresco*
Mantegna's fascination with Albertia perspective led him to produce the first full-blown illusionistic room scheme: the Painted Room in the Gonzaga Palace. The room's crowning achievement is the daring ceiling "oculus" – a painted opening giving way to an illusionistic summer sky. Servants and ladies of the court peep over its rim and seem to poke gentle fun at spectators below. One places her hand on a rod supporting a potted plant, as if she were about to roll it away. The fun is shared by winged infants, drastically foreshortened in a technique that became known as *di sotto in su* ("from below upward").

The perspective of the oculus is constructed according to the upward gaze of an observer standing directly below

Infants' heads poke through "holes"

Mantegna "shows off" by foreshortening back and front views

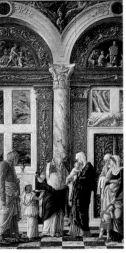

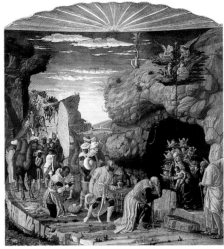

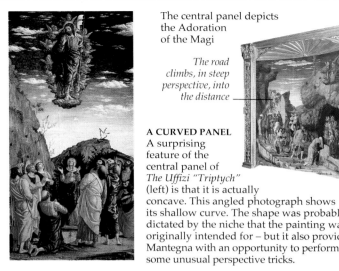

The central panel depicts the Adoration of the Magi

The road climbs, in steep perspective, into the distance —

A CURVED PANEL
A surprising feature of the central panel of *The Uffizi "Triptych"* (left) is that it is actually concave. This angled photograph shows its shallow curve. The shape was probably dictated by the niche that the painting was originally intended for – but it also provided Mantegna with an opportunity to perform some unusual perspective tricks.

Artists need to observe a real-life reclining model, so that they can understand, for instance, how the chest rises and obscures the neck from view

THE UFFIZI "TRIPTYCH"
Andrea Mantegna; c.1464;
overall size: 33¾ x 63½ in (86 x 161.5 cm); tempera on wood
The central panel is dominated by a great swath of rocky road. Seen from the center, this forcefully projects from the ground plane, and the picture surface magically disappears from view. Spectators feel that they can step onto the road's surface as it sweeps toward them and join the three kings as they pay homage to the Virgin and Child. On the right, a deep grotto, curving around the holy figures, takes on a powerful realism.

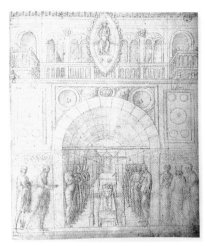

The units diminish just like squares in Alberti's pavement (pp. 7, 13). The irregular three-dimensional sections of the body they contain, however, demand more subtle calculation

FATHERLY INFLUENCE -
Mantegna was influenced by the sketchbooks of his father-in-law, Jacopo Bellini, which show a similar passion for perspective schemes. In Bellini's *Death of the Virgin*, c.1450 (right), Mary's foreshortened body anticipates Mantegna's *Dead Christ* (below).

PERSPECTIVE FORESHORTENING
Mantegna's masterful foreshortenings were probably based on studies from life as well as perspective principles. The theory is most easily understood if the figure is encased in a gridlike "box" divided into equal units along the length of its back. When the box is laid on the ground, with the figure's feet foremost, the units diminish as they recede (see diagram 8, p. 62).

Lamentation Over the Dead Christ

ANDREA MANTEGNA *c.1480*
26¾ x 31¾ in (68 x 81 cm); distemper on canvas
In this celebrated painting, the dead Christ is shown in a dramatically foreshortened pose, with his heavy head propped up by a pillow so that his majestic features can be clearly contemplated. His feet project beyond the marble slab and out of the picture space, forcing the viewer to focus on his gaping wounds, which are painted with a disturbing three-dimensionality. The perspective effect in the painting is so overwhelming that a viewer moving away from the painting seems to be followed by the figure.

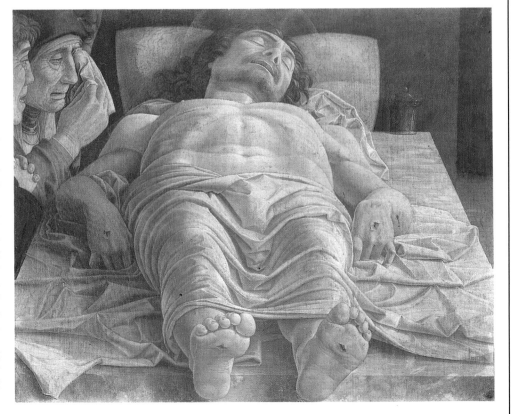

Art for art's sake

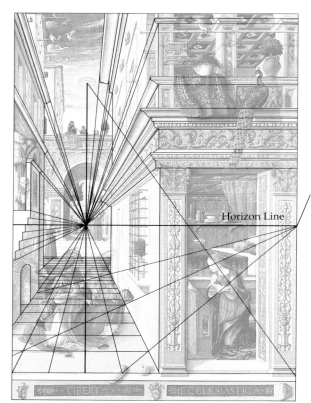

THE RENAISSANCE ENTHUSIASM for perspective was not simply due to a desire to imitate nature. It also coincided with a time when the status of painting was being raised from a medieval craft to one of the noblest professions, and the artist's skill had become a precious commodity. Painters could display this skill through beautifully constructed perspectives and clever foreshortenings that demonstrated art's mathematical basis. Carlo Crivelli's *Annunciation* is a flamboyant display of his perspective expertise and his love of material splendor, creating an idealized, but compellingly "real," version of the natural world.

Dish-shaped halo

TECHNICAL DETAILS
Crivelli shows off his foreshortening skills by making the angel Gabriel's halo a shallow dish rather than a simple ring. He even shows how the halo is attached to Gabriel's head!

DIVINE LOGIC
The theme of the Annunciation (when Gabriel appeared to Mary) was often an excuse for a dazzling perspective display, as it usually demanded an elaborate architectural setting. In such compositions, the perspective becomes almost symbolic. Here, the perspective focus – the centric ray from the viewer's eye to the vanishing point – is paralleled by the way the "eye" of the heavens (directly above the vanishing point) emits a ray. It is on this ray that the dove of the Holy Ghost descends, through a hole in the palace wall, to the Virgin. The perspective therefore helps to focus the eye on the "moment" of Christ's Incarnation as the Son of God. (Right: the vanishing point is where most of the lines converge.)

BALANCING ACT
High up on a bridge in the middle distance, Gabriel's holy message is wittily echoed by a message that has just been delivered by carrier pigeon. The pigeon's cage, a potted plant, and a book are precariously balanced on the ledge – an amusing trick borrowed from Mantegna (p. 20). A richly patterned rug, casting a heavy shadow, completes the illusion of reality.

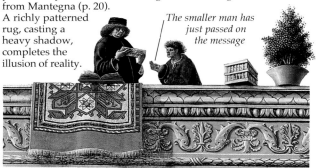

The smaller man has just passed on the message

LEADING THE EYE
The perspective cleverly focuses the eye on narrative detail. We can follow the line of sight of the man shielding his gaze along an orthogonal (see glossary) directly to the opening through which the Holy Spirit passes.

Horizon Line

Distance point (see glossary)

CHECKBACK LINES
The lines drawn through the corners of the floor tiles to the edge of the picture show that the perspective is correct. Crivelli would have used such lines as checkbacks when he was finalizing the perspective construction (as in Alberti's method; pp. 12–13).

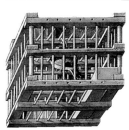

With characteristic showmanship, Crivelli includes a second bird cage, painted from a different angle than the one on the bridge

DECEIVING THE EYE
The illusionistic stone step in the foreground emphasizes the architectural framework of the composition and divides our world from the picture space. It also provides a surface for two surprising items – a gourd (despite its strange shape!) and an apple. Crivelli gives them strong shadows so that the viewer might, for a moment, think they are real. Their prominence is explained by their symbolic significance: a gourd is a symbol of Christ's Resurrection; the apple refers to man's fall from grace and his subsequent redemption.

Crivelli has added his signature to the center pilaster

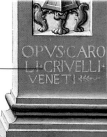

OPVS·CARO LI·CRIVELLI· VENETI

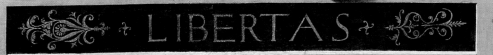

LIBERTAS

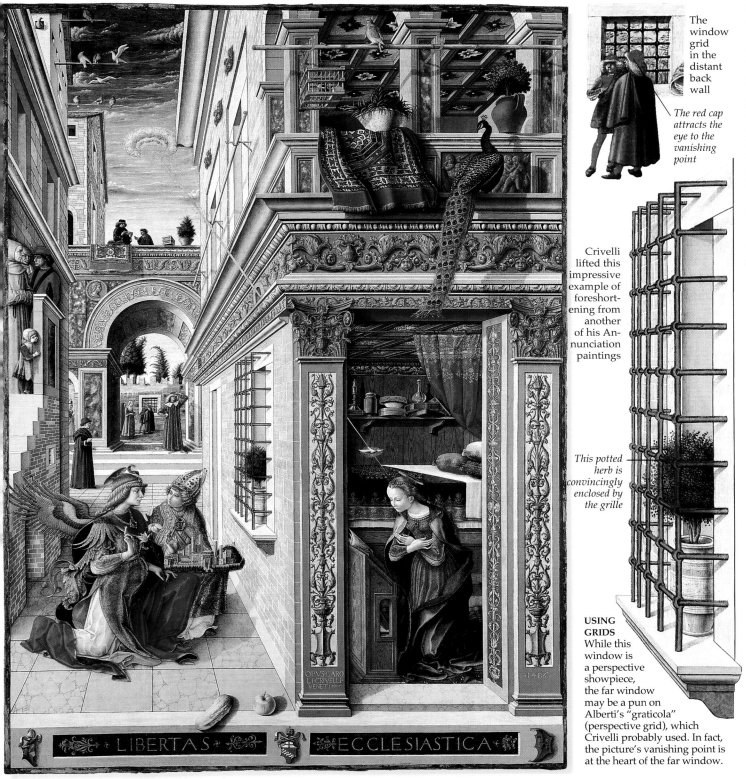

The
window
grid
in the
distant
back
wall

*The red cap
attracts the
eye to the
vanishing
point*

Crivelli
lifted this
impressive
example of
foreshort-
ening from
another
of his An-
nunciation
paintings

*This potted
herb is
convincingly
enclosed by
the grille*

**USING
GRIDS**
While this
window is
a perspective
showpiece,
the far window
may be a pun on
Alberti's "graticola"
(perspective grid), which
Crivelli probably used. In fact,
the picture's vanishing point is
at the heart of the far window.

LIBERTAS ⁘ ECCLESIASTICA ⁘

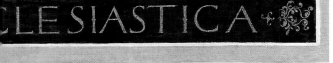

CLESIASTICA ⁘

The Annunciation, with Saint Emidius

CARLO CRIVELLI *1486; 6 ft 9 in × 4 ft 11 in (2.1 × 1.5 m); egg tempera & oil on canvas*
Crivelli's altarpiece for San Annunziata at Ascoli also marks an
important civic event of 1482. Standing on a bridge, between the
vanishing point and the eye of heaven, a town dignitary reads a
message stating that the Pope has granted Ascoli limited rights
of self-government. The message arrived on the Feast Day of
the Annunciation, and so the angel Gabriel is joined by Ascoli's
patron saint, Emidius, holding a wonderful model of the town.

23

Leonardo's explorations

THE WIDE-RANGING GENIUS of Leonardo da Vinci (1452–1519) embraced mathematics, philosophy, architecture, engineering, sculpture, science, and music, as well as painting. A passion for scientific truth lay at the heart of his intelligence: "Those who are enamored of practice without science," he wrote, "are like sailors who board a ship without rudder and compass, never having any certainty as to whither they go." In painting, linear perspective was the "rein and rudder," and Leonardo explored every facet of the system, even developing a theory of perspective distance based on proportions that echoed musical intervals. Through studying "natural" perspective – the way space and distance are actually perceived by the eye – he became preoccupied with weaknesses in Alberti's system (pp. 12–13). For example, he examined wide-angle vision and defined atmospheric perspective (pp. 28–29). Along the way, he investigated the role of the "camera obscura" in art (p. 43) and experimented with perspective curiosities such as anamorphosis (p. 32).

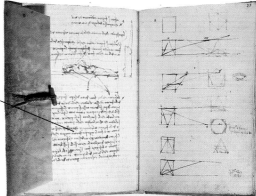

The artist's famous back-to-front writing

WRITINGS ON PERSPECTIVE
Leonardo's *Treatise on Painting* – a collection of manuscripts dating from 1473 to 1518 – includes a detailed section on linear perspective (1492). On one of the pages (shown above), Leonardo illustrates his method for transferring a figure onto the sides of a curved vault – a revolutionary technique that formed the basis of later illusionistic, or *trompe l'oeil*, decoration (wall and ceiling paintings that "deceive the eye").

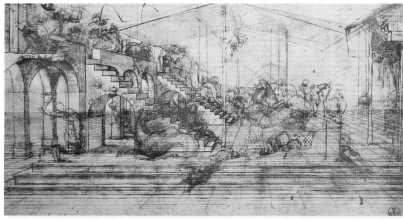

FOLLOWING ALBERTI'S PROCEDURE
This study for Leonardo's unfinished painting *The Adoration of the Magi* (1481) is an impressive display of one-point linear perspective. The foreground figures of the Madonna and Child and three kings, and a crowd of spectators, have been omitted – revealing the bare bones of the perspective construction. The foreshortened squared pavement recedes perfectly toward an off-center vanishing point – located on the head of the man riding the rearing horse. The angle of vision, however, is so wide that distant pavement squares on the far right and left are impossibly distorted.

"CURVILINEAR PERSPECTIVE"
Leonardo developed a new type of perspective based on the fact that the human field of vision is actually curved. He took the example of three circular columns (C), placed parallel to the picture plane. Where lines drawn from the edges of the columns to the eye are cut by a straight line (L), the outer columns appear wider than the central one. But where they are cut by an arc (A), they keep the same size.

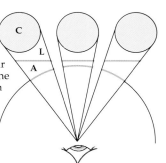

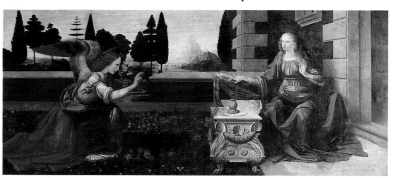

THE ANNUNCIATION
Leonardo; c.1472; 3 ft 2½ in x 7 ft 1½ in (0.98 x 2.17 m); tempera (?) on wood
This early work reveals a carefully worked out perspective framework. The strong diagonals of the Virgin's lectern (reading desk) and the tiled stone threshold recede properly toward the distant mountains. Incised lines beneath the paint surface show that even the top of the lectern's pedestal has been meticulously divided into squares so that Leonardo could find its center. The figures, however, are disproportionately large and are not as correct as they might at first seem.

EXTENDED TOO FAR
On close inspection, the Virgin's right arm is too long for her body. It is awkwardly elongated so that she can reach the pages of the book – which contain the famous prophecy of Isaiah (7:14): "A young woman is with child, and she will bear a son."

STORYTELLING PRIORITIES
When the scene is re-created in plan, and divided into squares, it is clear that the Virgin's arm and the lectern should move back a unit, in order to align the Virgin's arm properly with the rest of her body. Leonardo, however, is more interested in telling the story clearly (ensuring that the viewer focuses on the Virgin's expressive gestures) than in total perspective accuracy.

"Corrected" arm position
Arm position in painting

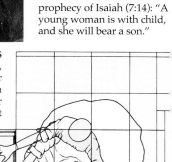

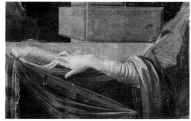

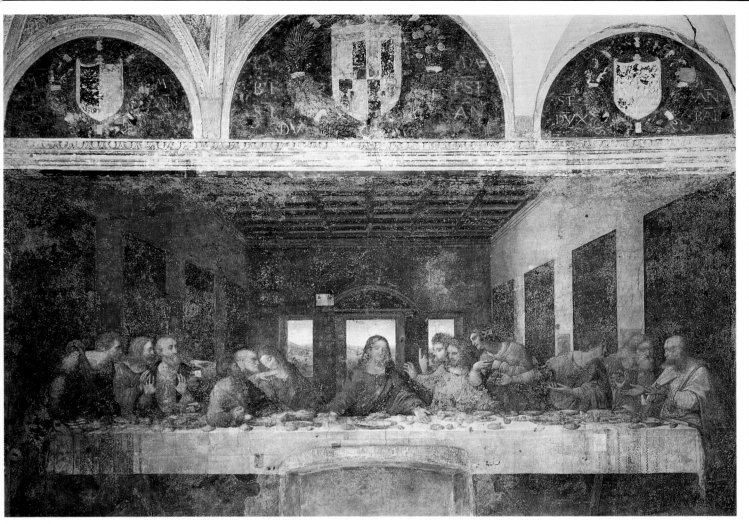

The Last Supper *(including semicircular lunettes)*
LEONARDO DA VINCI
c.1497; 15 ft x 28 ft 10 in (4.60 x 8.80 m); tempera and oil over ground limestone

Leonardo's magnificent *Last Supper* occupies the north wall of the refectory (monastic dining room) of the Convent of Santa Maria delle Grazie, Milan. It is placed high, because the refectory entrance was immediately below, and is designed to look like a deep upper room or annex. As the abbot blessed the food from his table at the other end of the refectory, he would have felt Christ presiding over the meal. A commanding sense of Christ's spiritual and physical presence derives partially from the fact that he is painted on a larger scale than his disciples, while the painting's illusionistic effects work through the power of perspective suggestion (below and right) rather than total perspective logic.

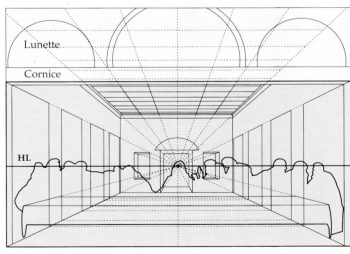

IMPOSSIBLE VIEWPOINT
For *The Last Supper* to seem like an extension of the refectory, the vanishing point – which is on Christ's right eye – should be lower, at the spectator's eye level. Instead, it is about 15 ft (4.5 m) above the floor level. The strong pull of the perspective, however, "lifts" the viewer from the floor to the correct viewpoint – a strangely spiritual phenomenon.

PERSPECTIVE PARADOXES
The perspective of *The Last Supper* is full of ambiguities. Leonardo uses it to create a deep room, but then denies the impression of space by placing the table "friezelike" across the top of it (to cover what would have been a strangely sloping floor). The table is so wide that there is no room for chairs at either end; the disciples are crowded around the far side – an undulating sea of heads grouped along the horizon line (HL). The coffered ceiling in the painting, suggesting a space leading directly off the refectory, does not in fact abut the architectural cornice, but it looks as though it could continue behind it, over the lunettes. Strong orthogonals draw the eye to the majestic head of Christ – who inhabits the picture's vanishing point (the black dot) while also dominating its foreground.

Dürer's perspective aids

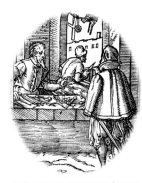

THE NUREMBERG ARTIST Albrecht Dürer (1471–1528) was famous primarily for his woodcuts and engravings. An artist with extraordinary natural gifts of imagination and observation, he nevertheless felt that art should have the "right foundations," and so he traveled broadly and immersed himself in Italian Renaissance art theory. In 1506, he visited Bologna to learn the art of "secret perspective," presenting his findings in his *Treatise on Measurement* (1525 and 1538) – a highly influential work that includes these fascinating illustrations of perspective devices.

DRAWING INSTRUMENTS
A compass shop in Dürer's Nuremberg, a town famous for its instrument-making.

YOUTHFUL ARDOR
This self-portrait of 1493 shows Dürer in the early years of his career. His intense expression confirms the opinion of a contemporary: "His only fault was a unique and infinite diligence ..."

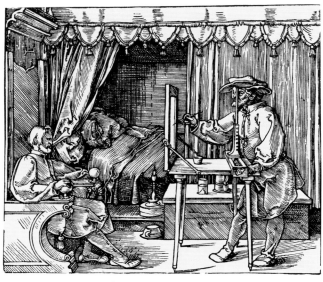

THE ARTIST'S GLASS *above*
The method of producing a scale image by tracing the outlines of an object on a sheet of glass appears in the writings of both Alberti and Leonardo da Vinci. It is still by far the easiest way to create a "perspective" – simply shut one eye and trace the view beyond your window on the windowpane. Dürer's woodcut illustrates a highly elaborate version: the framed glass plane is attached to a specially designed table complete with a mechanical eyepiece (adapted from contemporary surveying devices), which can be finely adjusted by means of a horizontal screw.

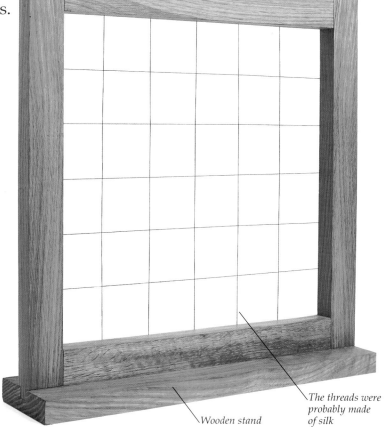

The threads were probably made of silk

Wooden stand

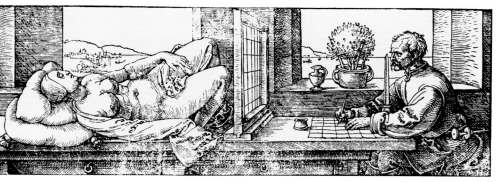

THE DRAFTSMAN'S NET *left and above*
Dürer's net (a reconstruction is shown above) is based on a similar device designed by Leonardo da Vinci, which was itself a variation on Alberti's grid (or "veil"). It consists of a squared net of black threads stretched over a sturdy wooden frame. An eyepiece, which fixes the artist's viewpoint, is positioned at a specific distance – twice the frame's height – from the device. The artist looks through the sight and copies the outlines of the model's form onto a squared drawing surface. Here, the net is placed very close to the model. This would have resulted in a sharply foreshortened pose.

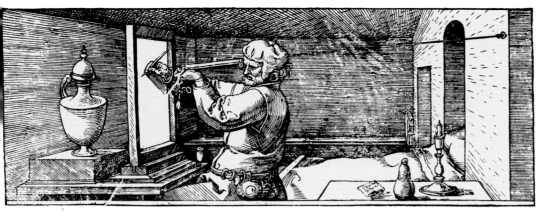

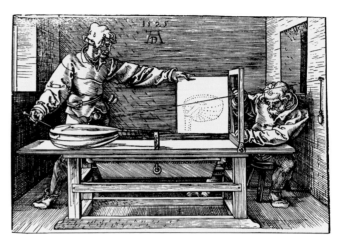

JACOB DE KEYSER'S INVENTION *left*

Dürer was highly impressed by de Keyser's new gun-style eyepiece. This compensated for the one drawback of the glass method – namely, that the artist's distance from the glass frame could never be greater than the reach of his arm. In de Keyser's device, the artist's "viewpoint" was fixed by the eye of a large needle inserted in the wall. This was joined by a silk string to a gun-sight-style instrument, with a pointed vertical element at the front and a peephole at the back. The artist "aimed" at the object and traced its outline on the glass, keeping the eyepiece aligned with the string to maintain the correct angle of vision.

DÜRER'S DEVICE *right and below*

Instead of an eyepiece, Dürer's own invention (reconstruction below) uses a needle fixed in the wall; the needle's eye represents the viewpoint. A string passes from this "eye," like a visual ray, through a frame, and ends in a pointer. The pointer's tip is placed on the part of the object on which the "eye" is focused – in this case a lute, being fore-shortened. The frame represents the picture plane and has two taut threads that can be moved so that they cross at the point where the string passes through. A hinged shutter with drawing paper attached is then swung inward, over the frame, so that this point – represented by the crossed threads – can be plotted.

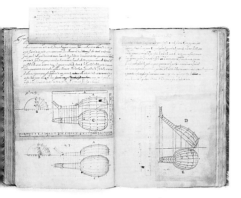

THE LUTE EXERCISE *above*

The foreshortened lute (see below) was a favorite topic of perspective treatises. In Ludovico Cigoli's unpublished *Practical Perspective* (c.1610–1613), shown here, the lute's shapely form is subjected to geometric analysis from every angle. This treatise, which was heavily influenced by Dürer, includes a lively section on perspective devices (p. 44).

DÜRER'S RULING PEN

This ruling pen was found under the floorboards of Dürer's house. Compared with his mechanical perspective aids, it is a straightforward instrument for ruling perspective lines. Dürer stressed the importance of mathematical precision when constructing perspectives, devoting a section of his treatise to a "Course in the Art of Measurement with Compass and Ruler."

PLOTTING POINTS

Using this frame was laborious; the whole process was repeated for every point on the object that the artist wished to record.

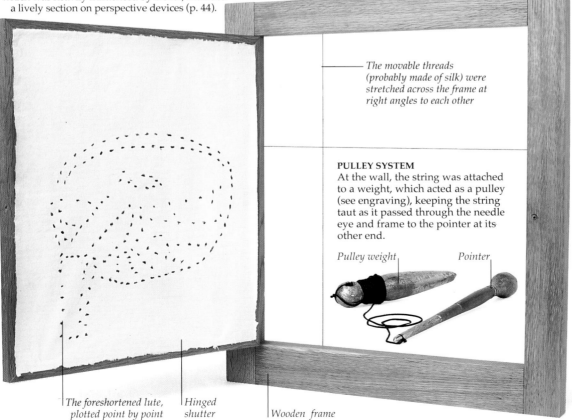

The movable threads (probably made of silk) were stretched across the frame at right angles to each other

PULLEY SYSTEM

At the wall, the string was attached to a weight, which acted as a pulley (see engraving), keeping the string taut as it passed through the needle eye and frame to the pointer at its other end.

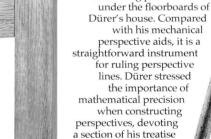

Pulley weight   *Pointer*

The foreshortened lute, plotted point by point | *Hinged shutter* | *Wooden frame*

Atmospheric perspective

FOR OUTDOOR SCENES, linear perspective cannot work without the aid of color and light, which play a crucial role in our perception of distance. This was acknowledged by Leonardo, who was the first to define atmospheric (or "aerial") perspective – a coloristic device well known to earlier artists. Atmospheric perspective is based on the optical effect caused by light being absorbed and reflected by the "atmosphere": a mist of dust and moisture. This mist is most dense at the Earth's surface, where it scatters light and causes distant tones to lose contrast. Blue light penetrates the mist most easily, making the sky appear blue and giving distant objects a bluish cast. For centuries, artists have mimicked this effect of nature, using cooler, paler tones toward the horizon.

ANCIENT VISTAS
Roman landscape painters understood what happens to light over distance, veiling forms in misty color, which cools toward shades of pale blue-gray.

Using blues

For the landscape (below) in the distance of *The Virgin of the Rocks*, Leonardo used the blue pigment azurite for the sea and sky, and ultramarine (purple-blue) for the rocks. The brownish underpainting was covered with lead white pigment in order to make the blues look more radiant.

Azurite

Lead white powder

Lapis lazuli, from which ultramarine pigment is extracted

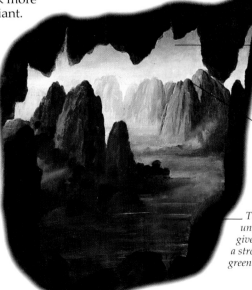

The sky becomes bluer to represent thinner air

Intense blue is applied where the rock peaks penetrate the upper atmosphere

The brownish underpainting gives these rocks a strong brown-green color

A detail from Leonardo's *Virgin of the Rocks*

The Virgin of the Rocks

LEONARDO DA VINCI
c.1508; 6 ft 2½ in x 3 ft 11¼ in (1.89 x 1.20 m); oil on wood
The remote landscape in this painting is a perfect example of aerial perspective. As the rocks recede, their color shifts from brown-green to the clear blue of the atmosphere. In the far distance, the bases of the rocks are obscured by the white, moisture-laden mists.

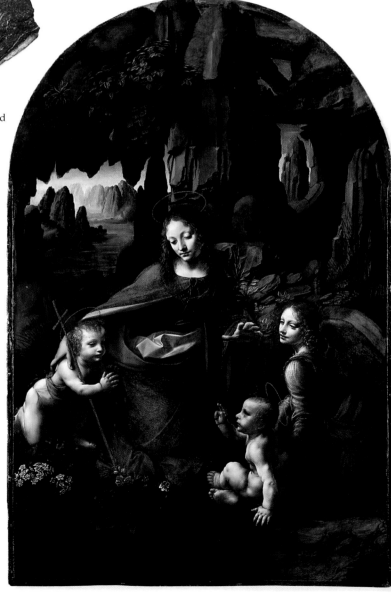

THE ART OF SUGGESTION

Chinese painting uses a type of atmospheric perspective in which the watery atmosphere dilutes background tones and dissolves distant forms. In this example Ming period, 1368–1644), faraway mountain peaks float in the sky, while their bases totally vanish. Distance is suggested as much by absence as by presence – one Chinese treatise states that: "If it exists above, it also exists below." The actual forms depicted – rocks, mountain, and trees – are the same as those shown by other cultures, but the vision of space and light is specifically Chinese. Viewers can lose themselves in the misty middle distance, using the image for quiet meditation.

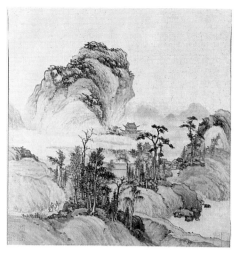

The Renaissance rediscovery of aerial perspective was due to the study of light and vision. But the effect could only be fully realized by painters who exploited the qualities of the "new" oil medium: pigment (powdered color) mixed with oil. (Oils began to gain dominance over tempera – pigment in a medium of egg, glue, or water – in the late 1400s.) Oils dry more slowly than tempera, so extra color can be added and blended. With tempera, darker color has to be added to indicate areas in shadow, whereas tinted glazes can be used over oils to tone down colors, creating subtler shadows. This means that truly atmospheric effects can be achieved in oil, such as an almost imperceptible blueing of colors toward the horizon. By J.M.W. Turner's time, the oil medium had been refined and there was a vast choice of pigments. Turner's paint box shows some of the main colors he used, including his favorite shade of yellow.

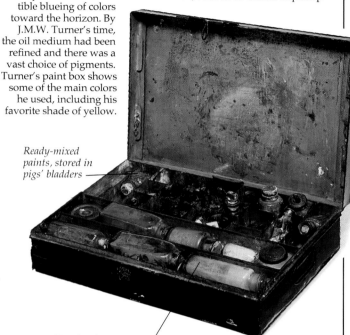

Ready-mixed paints, stored in pigs' bladders —

Powdered pigments, stored in bottles /

CANON BERNARDINUS DE SALVIATIS AND THREE SAINTS *left*
Gerard David; c.1501; 40½ x 37¼ in (103 x 94.5 cm); oil on oak

This Gerard David painting shows how 15th- and 16th-century artists often used broad color "bands" to create an atmospheric effect of distance – painting the background landscape an extremely bright blue. The middle ground was frequently a greenish tone, while the foreground was an earthy red-brown. This three-stage progression from warm to cool tones gives a basic impression of landscape depth. Later landscape painters, like Claude Lorrain, used this approach as a starting point, although each band contained infinite tonal gradations (p. 44).

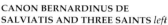

Norham Castle, Sunrise

J.M.W. TURNER *c.1845–50*
35¾ x 48 in (91 x 122 cm); oil on canvas

In this painting, translucent colors float over a thick white ground, giving the forms an "unearthly" delicacy. Turner has caught how, at sunrise, the cool ground fills the air with moisture, which scatters light and seems to unify earth and sky. Turner disliked grass green; the warm colors he chose instead still suggest the way early morning light reflects off damp fields. He used yellow to suggest the shimmering dominance of white light, and blues for the pale distance. The effect of space and depth is marred only by the castle: its well-defined solid mass makes it project forward, although it should fade away because it is actually in the far distance.

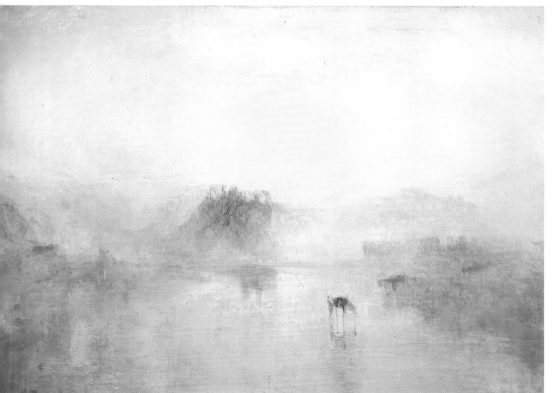

Room with a view

THE SALONE DELLE PROSPETTIVE, a great hall on the first floor of the Villa Farnesina in Rome, is one of the most ambitious illusionistic room schemes of the Renaissance. It was painted between 1517 and 1518 by the architect, painter, and stage-set designer Baldassare Peruzzi (1481–1536), who drew on his theatrical expertise and his knowledge of classical wall painting to create a decoration to rival the villas of Ancient Rome. The room's name comes from its imaginary architectural perspectives, which seem to "open up" the walls. These perspectives extend the room on all four sides with imposing porticoes (covered walkways) leading to low "stone" balconies, from which can be seen wonderful landscape views.

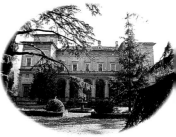

THE VILLA FARNESINA
Peruzzi was the architect of the Villa Farnesina, built for the Pope's banker, Agostino Chigi. Its site, on the Tiber River near the Porta (Gate) Settimiana, features strongly in Peruzzi's frescoes inside the villa.

Salone delle Prospettive

BALDASSARE PERUZZI *Villa Farnesina, Rome; 1517–18; fresco*
Peruzzi's room is designed to be seen, as here, from the center of the exterior wall. Viewed from this position, the floor squares painted on the walls continue logically from those on the actual floor of the room, out to the painted balconies, and the columns are properly aligned. The effect is enhanced by the clever imitation of precious marbles and the lively handling of luminous expanses of summer sky.

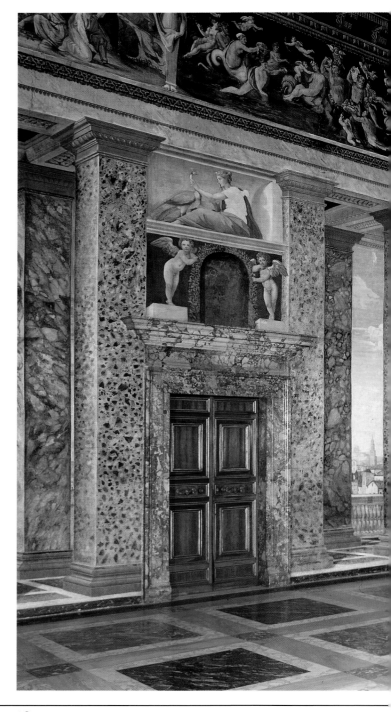

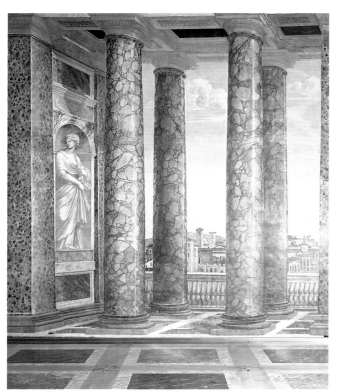

CENTRAL DISTORTION
The Salone delle Prospettive is usually photographed from the center of the room, as it has been here. This viewpoint is not, however, the center of the perspective construction. Viewed from the center of the room, everything is askew: the marble floor suddenly veers off at an angle, and the gilded capitals of the columns tilt alarmingly. The illusion of space and depth is still intact, but the architecture is no longer convincing.

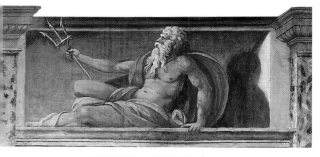

SCULPTURAL FIGURES *above*
Every aspect of the room is given the illusionistic treatment – from false niches containing figures painted in monochrome (one color) to imitate sculpture, to figures of the gods reclining above the windows and doors. Here Neptune, ensconced in his false stone recess, casts a strong, dark shadow that adds to the dramatic effect.

ANCIENT SCENE-PAINTING *right*
Peruzzi was highly influenced by the scenographic wall paintings of Ancient Rome. "The Room of the Masks," shown here, from the palace of Augustus, on Rome's Palatine Hill, is a particularly famous example. The perspective of such scenes was so skillful that, according to a story told by Pliny the Elder, birds tried to alight on the architecture, thinking that it was real.

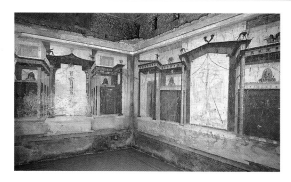

In the main picture, this detail is just to the left of the right-hand corner of the room

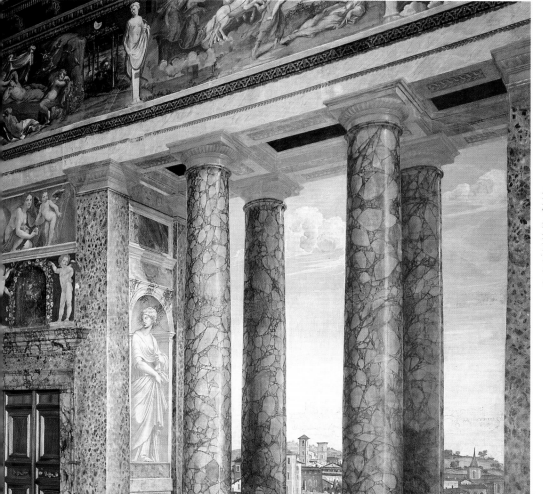

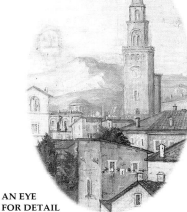

AN EYE FOR DETAIL
The landscapes in Peruzzi's Salone are freely painted in a spontaneous style derived from Roman frescoes. They have a freshness and intimacy enlivened by his eye for detail – note the wash hanging out to dry in the foreground.

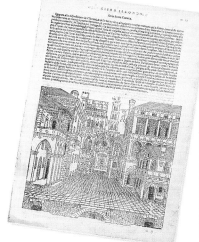

THEATRICAL PERSPECTIVE
Peruzzi was a gifted theatrical designer, and his Salone has often been compared to a stage set, complete with "wings" and decorative landscape "backdrop." Some idea of his work in this field can be gauged from the perspective stage designs of his pupil, Sebastiano Serlio. Serlio's *Second Book of Architecture* (1566) features designs – such as this "comic scene" – thought to be based on the work of Peruzzi.

Hidden messages

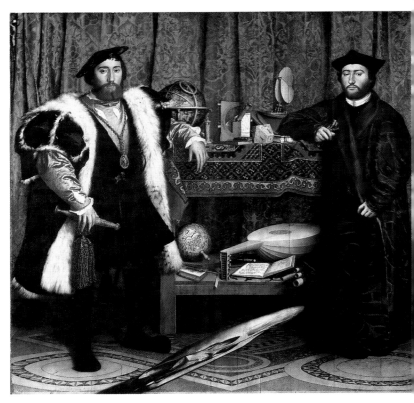

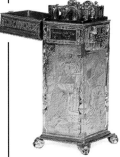

PERSPECTIVE GAMES
A fine 16th-century case of drawing instruments – Holbein's technical "games" were executed with mathematical precision.

An "anamorphosis" (from the Greek word meaning "transform") refers to a deliberately distorted image which, when viewed head on, is almost unrecognizable. It is only when the image is viewed from a certain angle that it suddenly assumes a normal appearance. This bizarre use of perspective was first described in the notebooks of Leonardo da Vinci, although the term "anamorphosis" was not coined until the 17th century. At first, it was probably used as a witty exercise, a perspective trick to display the artist's technical expertise. But soon, painters such as Hans Holbein (1497/8–1543) used anamorphosis in a more intellectual fashion, to conceal spiritual or political meanings in their works.

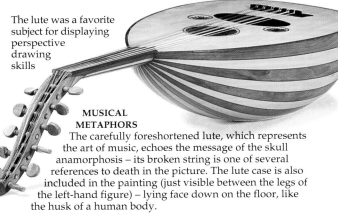

The lute was a favorite subject for displaying perspective drawing skills

MUSICAL METAPHORS
The carefully foreshortened lute, which represents the art of music, echoes the message of the skull anamorphosis – its broken string is one of several references to death in the picture. The lute case is also included in the painting (just visible between the legs of the left-hand figure) – lying face down on the floor, like the husk of a human body.

IN THE SHADOW OF DEATH
The grossly distorted skull looms across the mosaic floor of Holbein's painting like some strange lunar landscape. Just like the cryptic code to a secret message, it begs to be deciphered – and all the clues are there. Spectators viewing *The Ambassadors* must simply discover the improbable viewpoint – about 6½ ft (2 m) to the right of the edge of the painting, at the eye level of the two ambassadors – to unscramble the skull image and so understand its symbolic meaning. That said, there was no record of this strange image as an anamorphosis until 1873 – over three centuries after the picture was painted!

The Ambassadors

HANS HOLBEIN THE YOUNGER
1533; 6 ft 9 in x 6 ft 10½ in (2.06 x 2.10 m); oil on wood
This celebration of man's intellectual and spiritual powers is also a commentary on the frailty of human endeavors. Jean de Dinteville (left) and a fellow diplomat, Georges de Selve, are shown against a backdrop of objects relating to the pursuit of learning. The globe (lower shelf), to which Holbein added the name of Dinteville's French estate, refers to his worldly domain; the skull is a stark reminder of man's mortality and spiritual concerns.

A NOTE OF HOPE *above*
A silver crucifix peeping out of the top left-hand corner symbolizes the afterlife. Holbein painted it sideways to show off his technical skill.

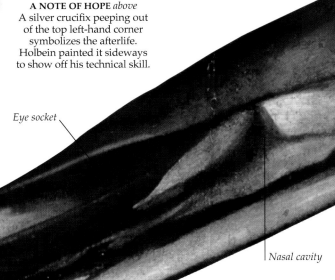

Eye socket

Nasal cavity

Constructing an anamorphosis

An anamorphic image is an extreme case of perspective, where the viewpoint is at the side, and near the plane, of the picture itself. First, a squared grid is placed over a scale drawing of the undistorted image, to determine the key points of the design. ABCD defines the boundaries of the image, and a line drawn from B to D fixes the scale of the squares. The artist then draws a distorted grid, onto which the design is transferred – a side view in which the proportions are drastically altered, but the points of the grid fall on the same places in the design.

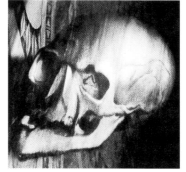

DEATH'S TRUE FACE
This photograph shows the skull in *The Ambassadors* as it suddenly appears when seen from the correct viewpoint. An effect of such perspectives is that the rectified image seems to float above the picture surface. The painting was possibly hung on a staircase in Dinteville's chateau, so that the corrected skull may have appeared from below left, or above right, as the viewer went up or down the stairs. Holbein would have used a distorted grid like the one below to create his macabre image.

Undistorted squared grid

Distorted grid

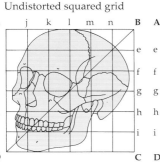

To see this skull corrected, view it at a shallow angle, from the right-hand side of the drawing

DRAWING THE DISTORTED GRID
The artist draws a vertical line to represent one edge of the original undistorted image (say, the left-hand edge AD), and places a point, X, at some distance to the right. Lines are then drawn that connect A, D, e, f, g, h, and i to X. The farther away X is from AD, the more the distorted image will be stretched. A second point, Y, is placed above X, and is joined to D. Where YD crosses AX, the point B is placed. Point C is set beneath B, on the line XD. Vertical lines are then drawn through the points where the lines that join e, f, g, h, and i to X intersect the line BD. These correspond to the grid lines marked j, k, l, m, and n. The skull design is now ready to be transferred and transformed!

Cranium

HOLBEIN'S SIGNATURE
The skull may be a pun on the artist's name: in German, *hohle bein* means "hollow bone." A death's head was also Dinteville's heraldic device.

Eye socket

Strange toys

In the 18th and 19th centuries, semicircular anamorphic images – often known as "curvilinear" because they consist of curved lines – were highly popular. The image appeared magically before the viewer's eyes in a cylindrical mirror – just as curved mirrors grossly distort normal images, so they can also make distorted images appear natural!

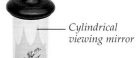

Cylindrical viewing mirror

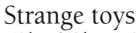

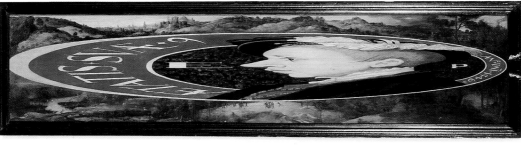

Viewing hole

Front view

Side view

PORTRAIT OF PRINCE EDWARD VI
William Scrots; 1546; 16¾ x 63 in (42.5 x 160 cm); oil on wood
This anamorphosis of Prince Edward VI of England (painted by a follower of Holbein, probably for the prince's amusement) superimposes the long-nosed, compressed head of a young boy on a panoramic landscape. When the picture is viewed from the right-hand edge (a chunk has been cut out of the frame for this), the head is transformed into a living likeness of Edward VI.

Works of reference

THE RICH COLLECTION of scholarly treatises that belonged to the 17th-century Spanish master Diego Velázquez (1599–1660) gives us a remarkable insight into his interest in visual illusion. His library in the Alcázar Palace in Madrid abounded in volumes on perspective, geometry, and optics – some of which are illustrated on the opposite page. The inventory of his equipment lists ten mirrors, which were probably used as compositional aids, two compasses, an instrument for "producing lines," and a "thick round glass" in a box – possibly an early form of camera obscura (pp. 42–43). Velázquez's late masterpiece *Las Meninas* ("The Maids of Honor") reveals how naturally he used this fund of perspective knowledge, combining subtle geometry with a breathtaking handling of shadow and light.

Las Meninas
DIEGO VELAZQUEZ
1656; 10 ft 5 in x 9 ft (3.2 x 2.8 m); oil on canvas
Here the perspective gives clues to the narrative. In the mirror on the back wall there is a reflection – of the Spanish king and queen. From the careful perspective it can be deduced that the large canvas at the front lies between the mirror and the figures it reflects – Velázquez is showing himself painting the king and queen's portrait! The little princess (center) and attendants are not looking at us, but at the king and queen posing at our side.

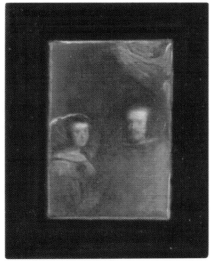

MIRROR IMAGE
Juxtaposing this blurred mirror image with a view of a man glimpsed through an open door – a common feature of illusionistic villa decoration – suggests that Velázquez is commenting on the nature of painted illusion.

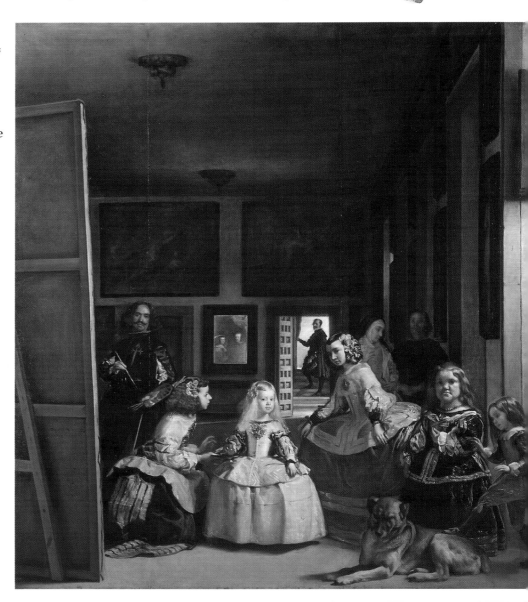

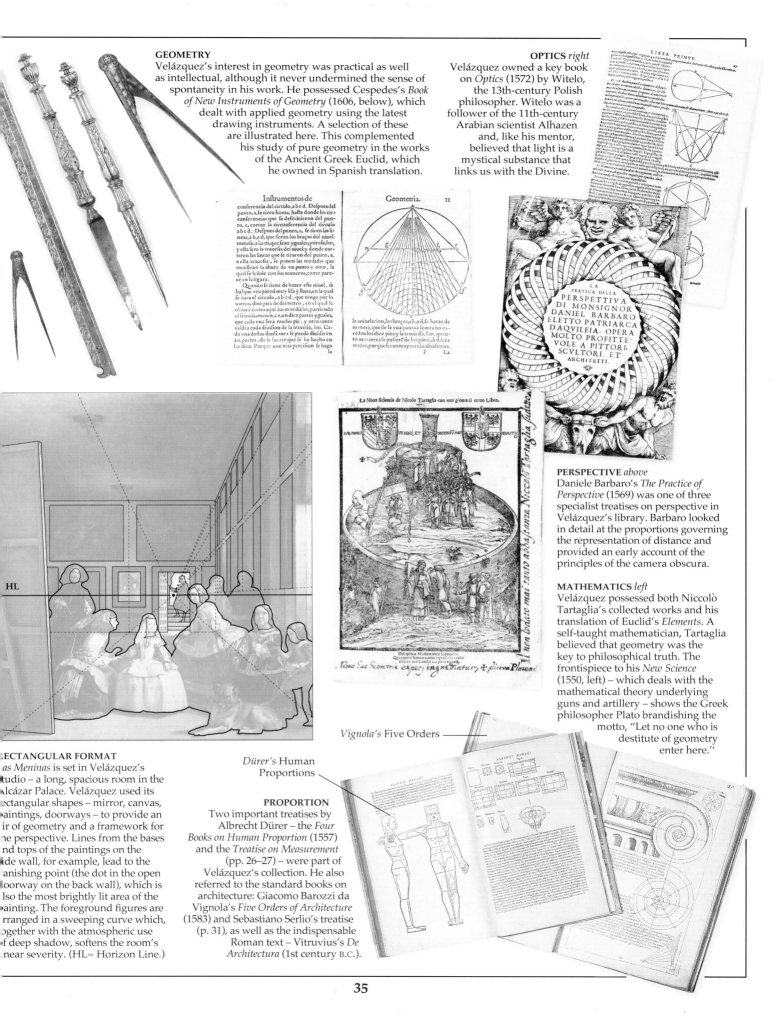

GEOMETRY
Velázquez's interest in geometry was practical as well as intellectual, although it never undermined the sense of spontaneity in his work. He possessed Cespedes's *Book of New Instruments of Geometry* (1606, below), which dealt with applied geometry using the latest drawing instruments. A selection of these are illustrated here. This complemented his study of pure geometry in the works of the Ancient Greek Euclid, which he owned in Spanish translation.

OPTICS *right*
Velázquez owned a key book on *Optics* (1572) by Witelo, the 13th-century Polish philosopher. Witelo was a follower of the 11th-century Arabian scientist Alhazen and, like his mentor, believed that light is a mystical substance that links us with the Divine.

PERSPECTIVE *above*
Daniele Barbaro's *The Practice of Perspective* (1569) was one of three specialist treatises on perspective in Velázquez's library. Barbaro looked in detail at the proportions governing the representation of distance and provided an early account of the principles of the camera obscura.

MATHEMATICS *left*
Velázquez possessed both Niccolò Tartaglia's collected works and his translation of Euclid's *Elements*. A self-taught mathematician, Tartaglia believed that geometry was the key to philosophical truth. The frontispiece to his *New Science* (1550, left) – which deals with the mathematical theory underlying guns and artillery – shows the Greek philosopher Plato brandishing the motto, "Let no one who is destitute of geometry enter here."

Vignola's Five Orders

Dürer's Human Proportions

RECTANGULAR FORMAT
Las Meninas is set in Velázquez's studio – a long, spacious room in the Alcázar Palace. Velázquez used its rectangular shapes – mirror, canvas, paintings, doorways – to provide an air of geometry and a framework for the perspective. Lines from the bases and tops of the paintings on the side wall, for example, lead to the vanishing point (the dot in the open doorway on the back wall), which is also the most brightly lit area of the painting. The foreground figures are arranged in a sweeping curve which, together with the atmospheric use of deep shadow, softens the room's linear severity. (HL= Horizon Line.)

PROPORTION
Two important treatises by Albrecht Dürer – the *Four Books on Human Proportion* (1557) and the *Treatise on Measurement* (pp. 26–27) – were part of Velázquez's collection. He also referred to the standard books on architecture: Giacomo Barozzi da Vignola's *Five Orders of Architecture* (1583) and Sebastiano Serlio's treatise (p. 31), as well as the indispensable Roman text – Vitruvius's *De Architectura* (1st century B.C.).

Hoogstraten's peepshow

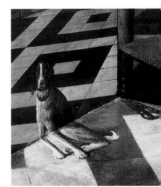

A PEEPSHOW IS A BOX with a painted interior which, when seen throug a small "peephole," seems to become a "real," three-dimensional scene. The miraculous world of Hoogstraten's peepshow is created through a masterly manipulation of simple central perspective and its distorted – or "anamorphic" (pp. 32–33) – form. His interior is viewed through two peepholes, which exactly control how spectators interpret what they see. Each peephole ensures that the viewer can only look with one eye, which confuses his or her judgment of scale and depth. It also means that images are viewed from precisely opposite the vanishing point of the painted panels inside, so that the distinction between real space and painted space disappears.

SAMUEL VAN HOOGSTRATEN
The Dutch master Hoogstraten (1627–1678) was a pupil of Rembrandt. His fame now rests on his perspective peepboxes.

Left peephole

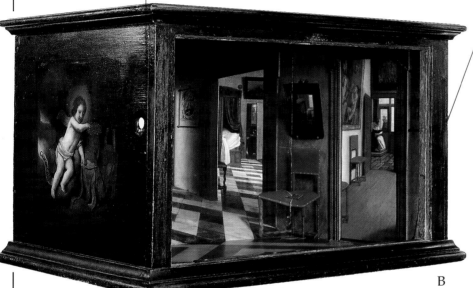

Location of right peephole

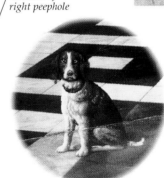

PEEPHOLE MAGIC
The dog sits across two panels (above) – its top half is painted undistorted but its bottom half is painted anamorphically. Whe this dog is seen at an angle through the right-hand peephole (left), the distortion is magically corrected

THE BACK PANEL (C
The floor on this panel is distorted because it is viewe obliquely from both peepholes. The rest of the right-han red chair is depicted on panel D (in ordinary perspective and anamorphically in the top-right corner of panel I

B

"Peepshow Box"

This open side may originally have been covered with translucent paper

SAMUEL VAN HOOGSTRATEN *late 1650s; box: 22⅜ x 34½ x 25 in (58 x 88 x 63.5 cm); oil paint (with some egg tempera and glue size); oak box*
The box displays two separate views (coinciding with the view from each peephole) of the interior of a Dutch house. The three-dimensional illusion is created from five panels painted with perspective scenes. The sixth side of the box is open, to let light in. This light source is incorporated into the design of the interior; the opening is imagined as a shuttered window, filtering bright pools of sunlight into the rooms.

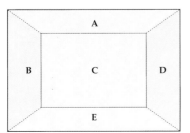

This plan shows which interior panels the captions refer to

THE LEFT-END PANEL (B)
This end panel can be seen from the right-hand peephole and is painted in single-point perspective with the peephole as its vanishing point. The amount of floor that is included, together with the width suggested by the perspective, make this end of the room seem much wider and farther away than the actual end of the box.

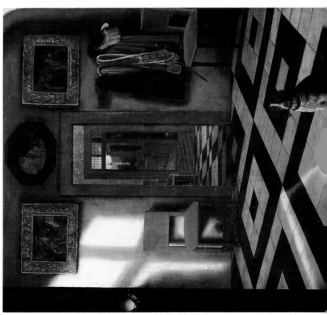

THE UNDERSIDE OF THE LID (A)

The beamed ceiling of the room is viewed conventionally from the right-hand peephole. The upper part of the right-hand wall (on the other half of the panel), however, is the only part visible from the left-hand peephole and is elongated because it is viewed obliquely.

A

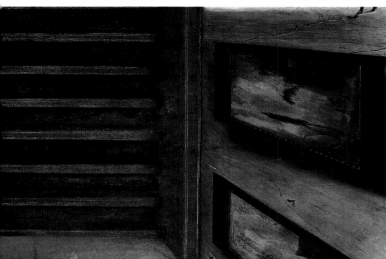

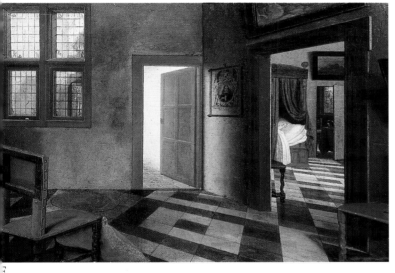

E

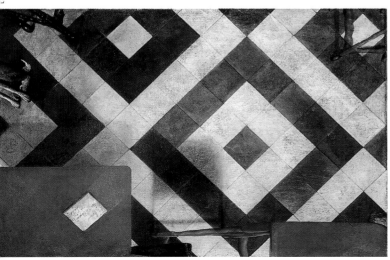

SAMUEL PEPYS DECEIVED

The celebrated diarist Samuel Pepys provides a record (right) of the impact that Hoogstraten's perspective scenes had. Pepys saw Hoogstraten's large painting *View Down a Corridor* (below right) at a house in London on January 26, 1663, where it hung behind a closet door. He was full of surprised admiration when, on opening the door, he saw that the vast corridor was, as he wrote, "only a plain picture on the wall."

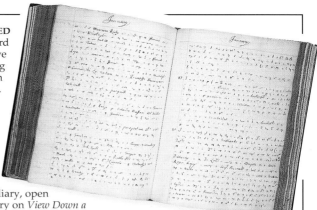

Pepys's diary, open to his entry on *View Down a Corridor*, written in shorthand

VIEW DOWN A CORRIDOR *right*
Hoogstraten; 1662
8 ft 8 in x 4 ft 5¾ in (2.64 x 1.36 m); oil on canvas
This painting now hangs at the end of a corridor – as the artist intended – in an English country house in Gloucestershire. The illusion of the corridor continuing comes from the powerful single-point perspective, and a subtle fading-out of color, light, and detail over distance.

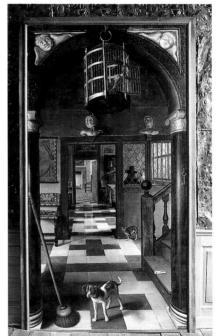

THE BASE PANEL (E)

Where the floor panel meets the framed open side of the box, Hoogstraten has painted the top of a chair back – and he has even hammered real studs along its edge!

THE RIGHT-END PANEL (D)

This doorway occupies the same plane as the right-hand wall of the box, but the top of the wall (painted on the underside of the lid), and the continuation of the left-hand side of this wall onto the back panel, make
D   the perceived space much higher and wider than the real space.

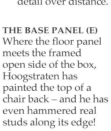

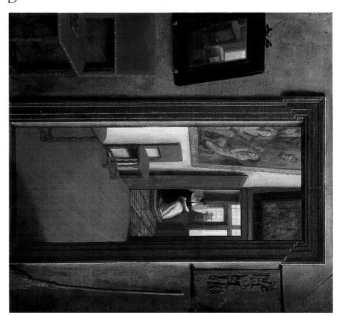

Dutch specialities

INGENIOUS PERSPECTIVE VIEWS were highly prized by the art-buying classes of 17th-century Holland. Those that recorded places and landmarks were especially popular, and many Dutch artists specialized in this area. In 1628, Pieter Saenredam (1597–1665) turned "completely to the painting of perspectives, church halls, galleries, buildings, and other such things ... from life," while Carel Fabritius (1622–54) became known as a master of illusionistic perspective. Even the landscapist Hobbema (1638–1709) used perspective to structure his most famous painting.

The Avenue, Middelharnis

MEINDERT HOBBEMA *1689; 40¾ x 55½ in (103.5 x 141 cm); oil on canvas*
Famous for its central perspective plan, this landscape draws the eye down the tree-lined avenue. In such deep perspectives, the foreground seems to turn as the viewer walks past the painting; as you move to the left, the path in the middle distance on the right swings into view.

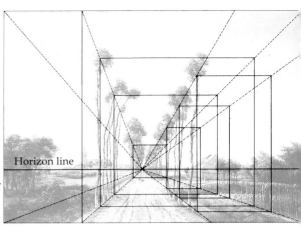

Horizon line

LANDSCAPE INTO DEPTH
Hobbema creates a deep perspective by foreshortening the ground plane so much that all the objects diminish rapidly in size. There is a clear horizon line, and the bases of the trees, and the dikes, recede to a distinct vanishing point. By placing this vanishing point – which also corresponds to the spectator's imagined viewing point – near the head of the man walking toward us, Hobbema makes viewers feel as though they are entering the landscape on the same avenue, and might meet the man. There were originally two extra trees, one on each side of the road, in the foreground. By deleting them, Hobbema opens up the landscape, giving it unusual airiness and depth.

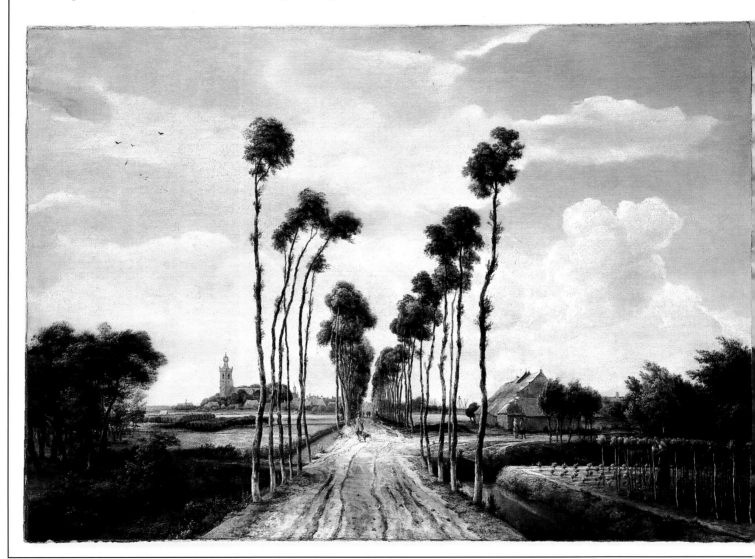

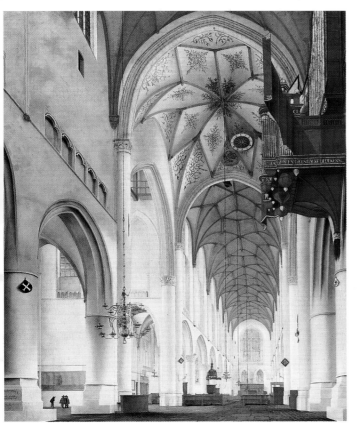

INTERIOR OF ST. BAVO'S CHURCH AT HAARLEM

Pieter Jansz. Saenredam; 1648; 69 x 56½ in (175 x 143.5 cm); oil on wood
Saenredam's method of creating convincing architectural
perspectives – such as this highly detailed painting of St. Bavo's
Church – was revolutionary in that he planned his paintings
according to the precise measurements of real buildings.
For this majestic interior of Haarlem's cathedral,
he used the dimensions of the building's floor
plan and elevation, which had been published
by the surveyor, Pieter Wils, specifically for
the use of artists. Saenredam then made
meticulous freehand drawings – on
which he recorded exact proportions and
distances – even noting his own height
from the cathedral floor, so that he knew
exactly where he should position the
horizon line of the painting.

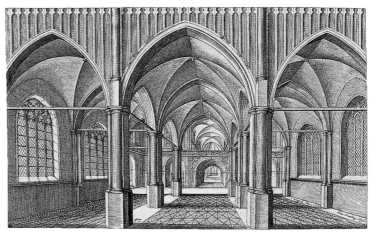

PRACTICAL PRINTS
Hans Vredeman de Vries's *Art of Perspective* (published 1604–05)
was hugely influential. It contained studies of imaginary architectural
interiors, which provided practical examples of specific perspective
effects for artists to imitate.

SURVEYING THE SCENE
Baldassare Lanci's adjustable "Universal
Instrument for Surveying and Perspective"
dates from 1557. As a perspective aid, it
was used in a horizontal position, with
an upright cylindrical drawing surface
attached around
half its rim. The artist
looked through the
sight arm, moving it
around as he took in the
scene. The drawing pin moved
with the sight arm, allowing
the key points of the design to
be pricked out on the inside of
the drawing surface.

Sight arm

Drawing pin

Holes for attaching drawing surface

Part of the surface engraving
shows the instrument in use

When the drawing
surface was detached
and flattened, the effect
may have been like
Fabritius's panoramic
view (left)

A VIEW OF DELFT
*Carel Fabritius; 1652; 6 x 12½ in (15.5 x
31.5 cm); oil on canvas laid down on walnut*
Rembrandt's pupil, Fabritius, may
have used aids to obtain his perspective
illusions. *A View of Delft* shows how
sophisticated his techniques could be.
The effect of this all-around view, which
suggests the natural sweep of the eye,
is like a wide-angle photograph. The
distorted architecture, the curves of the
ground plane, and the cut-off, heavily
foreshortened viola suggest that this
may have been designed as the curved
back panel of a triangular peepshow
(pp. 36–37) rather than as a painting.

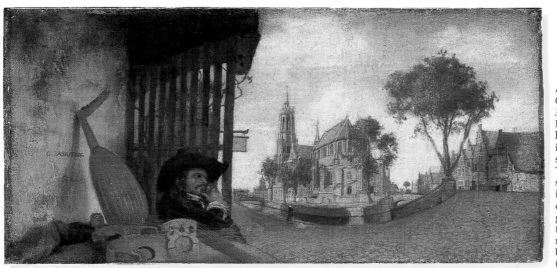

> **"** *[I intend] with a resolution to draw all the lines thereof to that true POINT, the Glory of God!* **"**
>
> Andrea Pozzo

Daring illusionism

T HE SPECTACULAR WORK of Andrea Pozzo (1642–1709), in the Church of S. Ignazio in Rome, represents the high point of perspective illusionism. The great dome, spanning the central aisle, is actually a flat, painted canvas, while the soaring architecture above the nave windows is equally fictitious. From the great distance of the viewer's position on the floor, the surface of the nave's vaulted ceiling miraculously dissolves into a breathtaking view of the heavens. The precision of the perspective is emphasized by the fact that there is only one perfect viewpoint for each illusion (marked by marble disks on the floor) – move to one side and both structures gracefully collapse!

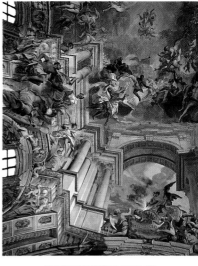

DESCENT INTO CHAOS
This corner of the ceiling is shown from a viewpoint located to the left-hand side of the nave on entering the church (see plan left). It shows how the figures begin to tumble from their perches and the columns seem to topple when the viewing position is incorrect. While some contemporaries saw this as a fault, Pozzo regarded it, on the contrary, as "an excellency of the work." Through the single-vanishing-point system, the "spirit" as well as the eye is drawn toward a central focus.

Vault of the Nave of S. Ignazio, Rome
("Allegory of the Missionary Work of the Jesuits")
ANDREA POZZO *1691–94; fresco*
The nave ceiling is designed to be seen from a disk on the floor, in the center of the nave. From there, the distinction between real and painted architecture disappears and the eye is swept up, through the swirl of figures, to the vanishing point – the Son of God.

Plan of S. Ignazio. A = entrance; B&C= correct viewing points on floor for ceiling (B) and dome (C); D = dome; X = spot from which distorted ceiling shot was taken

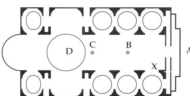

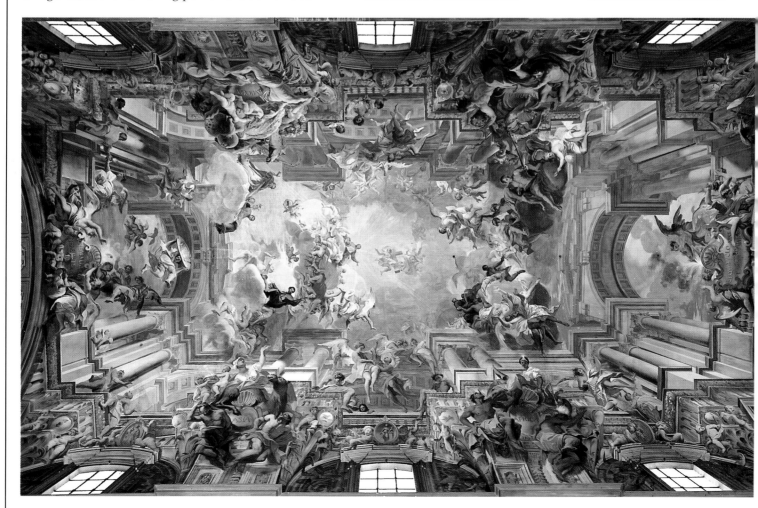

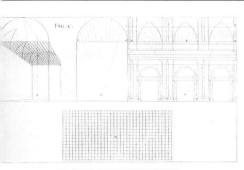

PROJECTION TECHNIQUE
In his two-volume treatise – *Perspective in Painting and Architecture* (1693 and 1700) – Pozzo explained the technique he used for the nave of S. Ignazio. First, he made a detailed drawing of the false architecture, and transferred it onto a squared grid. He then suspended a matching network of strings from the top of the nave, just below the curved vault. By stretching a string from the viewpoint (shown by black dots) through the suspended network, he could then project the grid onto the ceiling.

The Great Dome, S. Ignazio
ANDREA POZZO *1684–85; oil on canvas*
When the Jesuit church of S. Ignazio was built, it was meant to be crowned by an enormous dome, but the neighboring Dominican monks complained that it would deprive their library of light. The problem was solved, cheaply and effectively, by commissioning Pozzo to create a painted dome. The main picture shows how it appears when seen from the correct viewing point.

The play of "light" on "stone" is emphasized by the overall monochrome coloring of the dome

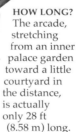

HOW LONG?
The arcade, stretching from an inner palace garden toward a little courtyard in the distance, is actually only 28 ft (8.58 m) long.

DISTORTED VIEW *left*
This shows how, from an incorrect viewpoint, the illusion crumbles. Pozzo's dome amazed everyone, but some architects criticized the painted architecture's "construction." Pozzo laughingly replied that a friend of his would bear "all damages and costs" should the dome ever fall down!

Perspective Arcade *Inner courtyard of Palazzo Spada, Rome*
FRANCESCO BORROMINI *c.1652–53; 28 ft 2 in (8.58 m) long*
Illusionistic games can also be played with real architecture. Here, a false impression of great depth is created by mimicking perspective effects: the columns literally get smaller the farther back they go, as do the ceiling coffers (panels); the floor slopes upward, and the cornices downward; the columns are thicker at the front than the back; and the "squares" on the pavement are actually trapezoids.

Cornice

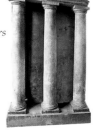

Coffers

HUMAN SCALE
A 6-ft (1.8-m) man shown at the back and front of the arcade shows the real scale of the architecture.

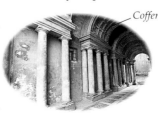

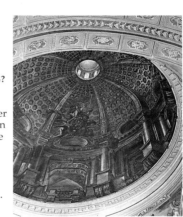

The magic eye

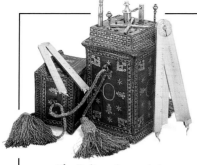

The Italian view-painter, Canaletto, made rigorous use of mathematical drawing devices

A CAMERA OBSCURA (meaning "dark chamber") is a device that can produce images of "magic" realism. It was originally a dark room or cubicle, with a pinhole in one side that allowed light rays from a sunlit view to enter. The rays crossed as they passed through the hole, then fanned out to form a reduced, upside-down image on a white wall or screen. The image was then corrected with a mirror and traced. Refinements soon appeared: built-in mirrors, prisms, and lenses angled light rays so that the image was focused and the right way up. By the 1700s, it had been reduced to a portable box, popular with amateur artists. Two painters, Vermeer (1632–75) and Canaletto (1697–1768), are consistently linked with its sorcery.

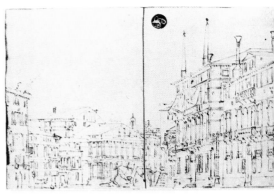

PREPARATORY STAGES
Some of Canaletto's preliminary sketches strongly suggest use of a camera obscura. In his "Accademia" sketchbook, drawings are often joined together to form a continuous scene (above). This can be compared with the way vacation snapshots are frequently pieced together to simulate a "wide-angle" effect (below). Like the photographer, Canaletto may have positioned his camera obscura and then turned it slightly to take two adjacent views.

The Grand Canal with San Simeone Piccolo

CANALETTO *c.1738; 4 ft 1 in x 6 ft 8½ in (1.25 x 2.05 m); oil on canvas*
In this Venetian view, the precise way the buildings recede in perspective and the subtle tonal gradations are "photographic" effects that point to the use of a camera obscura. The panoramic composition may confirm a contemporary remark that Canaletto used the aid to paint vistas "from more than one viewpoint."

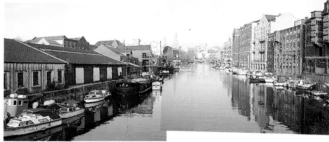

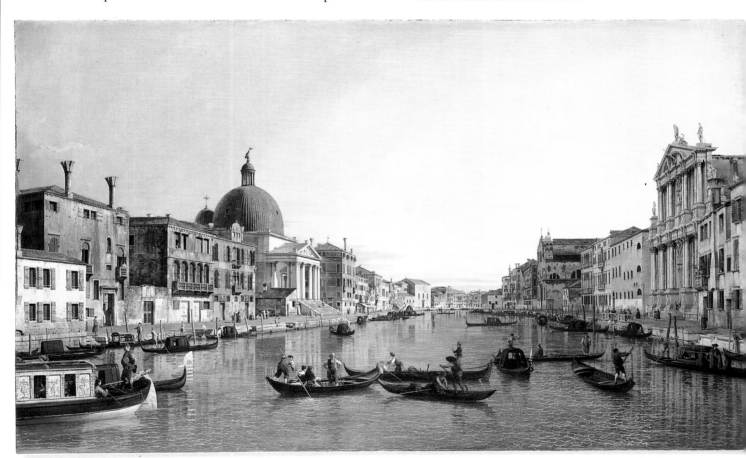

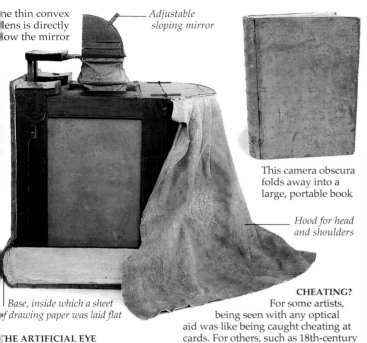

the thin convex lens is directly below the mirror

Adjustable sloping mirror

Hood for head and shoulders

Base, inside which a sheet of drawing paper was laid flat

This camera obscura folds away into a large, portable book

THE ARTIFICIAL EYE

The tent-type camera obscura was invented by the astronomer Kepler. Its revolving head made it perfect for painting views, and Canaletto may have used one. In this 19th-century example, a prism replaces the earlier lens and mirror combination, deflecting light rays into the tent and onto the drawing paper inside.

Rods rotate the prism to centre the image

The tent is raised on a tripod to a suitable working height

CHEATING?

For some artists, being seen with any optical aid was like being caught cheating at cards. For others, such as 18th-century painter Joshua Reynolds, the camera obscura's photographic images did not sit well with the lofty claims of "high" art. His camera obscura (above) folded away into the form of a book, so that it wasn't too obvious.

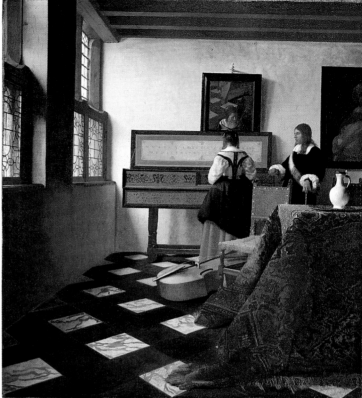

"The Music Lesson"

JAN VERMEER *1660s*
29 x 25½ in (73 x 64.5 cm); oil on canvas

Various effects in Vermeer's work provide evidence that he used a camera obscura. These include the "photographic" manner in which objects in the foreground (like the draped table and white jug above) loom in front of background objects and have sharply defined edges; the condensed perfection of the forms (due to the intensity of the reduced camera obscura image); and the brilliant, jewel-like colors.

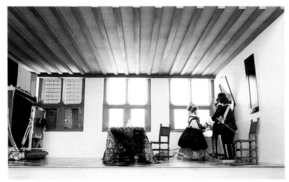

VERMEER'S ROOM *above & right*
Compelling evidence for Vermeer's use of a camera obscura comes from Philip Steadman's research into six Vermeer paintings that all show the same interior. From perspective clues in the paintings, he created a reconstruction of Vermeer's room (possibly his studio) with the furniture and figures from *"The Music Lesson."* Using the model, Steadman (seated on the right, as Vermeer) found that the viewpoints of all six pictures occupy the same area of the room. Also, if the angle of view of each painting is carried back through the viewpoint to the far wall, it forms a rectangle on the wall that is the precise size of each picture. This coincides with the way in which the lens in a cubicle-type camera obscura (right) projected an image onto the back wall.

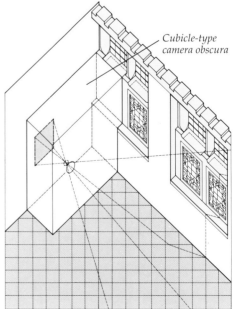

DRAWING UP THE DIMENSIONS *right*
Steadman's plan shows how the dark cubicle may have been set up, with a light aperture, focusing lens, and back screen. The camera obscura is represented in the model above by a plate camera, with its lens positioned at the viewpoint and its plate aligned with the back wall of the room.

Cubicle-type camera obscura

Ingenious devices

FROM THE 15TH century onward, a bewildering variety of devices were invented to help the artist create perfectly correct perspectives. They ranged from simple drawing aids, such as Alberti's "veil" (p. 26), to mechanical apparatus specially adapted from surveying and astronomical instruments, as well as sophisticated optical aids that were capable of producing vivid three-dimensional illusions. The more complex of these instruments, combining mirrors and lenses, led directly to the invention of the photographic camera (see camera obscura, pp. 42–43).

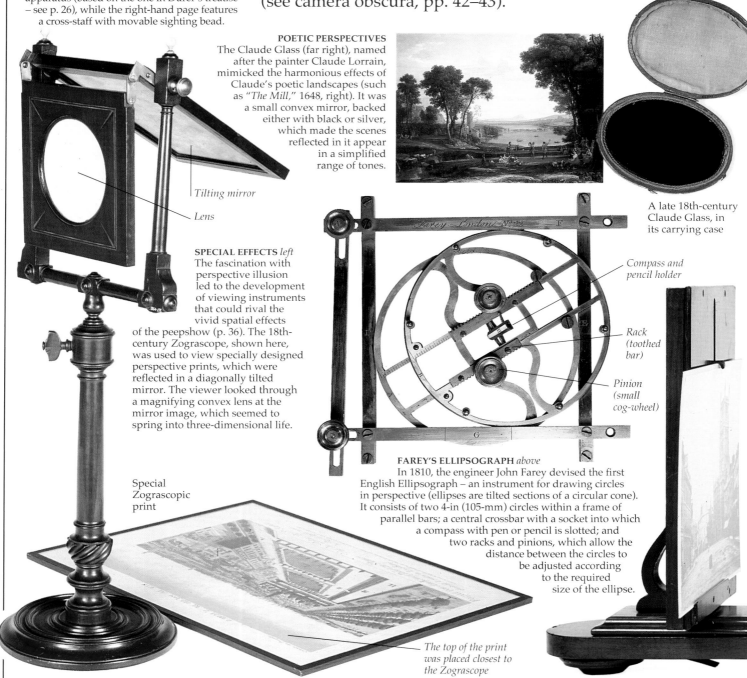

PRACTICAL GADGETS
Ludovico Cigoli's *Practical Perspective* (c.1610–1613) illustrates five perspective gadgets. The left-hand page shows a gun-style apparatus (based on the one in Dürer's treatise – see p. 26), while the right-hand page features a cross-staff with movable sighting bead.

POETIC PERSPECTIVES
The Claude Glass (far right), named after the painter Claude Lorrain, mimicked the harmonious effects of Claude's poetic landscapes (such as *"The Mill,"* 1648, right). It was a small convex mirror, backed either with black or silver, which made the scenes reflected in it appear in a simplified range of tones.

A late 18th-century Claude Glass, in its carrying case

Tilting mirror

Lens

SPECIAL EFFECTS *left*
The fascination with perspective illusion led to the development of viewing instruments that could rival the vivid spatial effects of the peepshow (p. 36). The 18th-century Zograscope, shown here, was used to view specially designed perspective prints, which were reflected in a diagonally tilted mirror. The viewer looked through a magnifying convex lens at the mirror image, which seemed to spring into three-dimensional life.

Compass and pencil holder

Rack (toothed bar)

Pinion (small cog-wheel)

Special Zograscopic print

FAREY'S ELLIPSOGRAPH *above*
In 1810, the engineer John Farey devised the first English Ellipsograph – an instrument for drawing circles in perspective (ellipses are tilted sections of a circular cone). It consists of two 4-in (105-mm) circles within a frame of parallel bars; a central crossbar with a socket into which a compass with pen or pencil is slotted; and two racks and pinions, which allow the distance between the circles to be adjusted according to the required size of the ellipse.

The top of the print was placed closest to the Zograscope

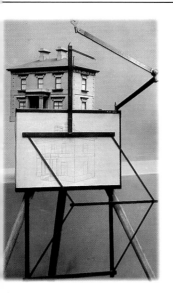

MECHANICAL APPARATUS *left*
The engineer James Watt devised an elaborate portable perspective system (1765) that was simple to use. The draftsman lined up the pinhole eyepiece (at the top right-hand corner of the drawing board) with a sight arm (sticking up vertically above the board). This arm was moved over the contours of an object, while a pencil (inserted at the arm's base) traced the corresponding outline on the drawing paper, and a framework of parallelograms kept the perspective proportions correct.

THE CAMERA LUCIDA *left*
W.H. Wollaston's Camera Lucida, patented in 1806, was a precise aid to perspective drawing. Closing one eye and looking down and over the edge of a four-sided prism, the artist could see the object in front of the apparatus, as well as the "three-dimensional" image of the object projected onto the drawing paper below.

One of the lenses used in the Graphic Telescope

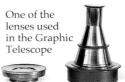

Two alternative eyepieces for the Graphic Telescope

Eyepiece – this can be adjusted so that the viewer can focus the image

Mirror

Circular opening to let light enter from outside

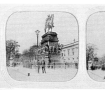

Left: The time lapse between these two views is seen by the fact that a boy appears (right) in place of the policeman (left)!

VICTORIAN STEREOSCOPIC PRINTS
These pairs of photographic images were used with stereoscopes designed by David Brewster. Like prints used with Charles Wheatstone's device (below right), they aimed to simulate the "stereoscopic" way in which human vision works (below). The two lower photos were taken simultaneously, with a double-lensed camera, but the upper photos were taken separately (a short distance apart), by an ordinary camera used to re-create the view of each eye.

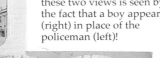

VARLEY'S GRAPHIC TELESCOPE
In 1809, English watercolorist Cornelius Varley created a challenge to the Camera Lucida with his Graphic Telescope. It was designed to help teachers of perspective and painters of landscape and architecture who wanted to produce detailed views of actual places. The device works like an ordinary telescope, using a combination of lenses. Light enters through an opening near one end and is reflected horizontally, via a mirror, through two convex lenses (one at each end of the telescope) and into the eyepiece. There, a second mirror bounces it upward into the viewer's eye, where it forms a "graphic" perspective image.

Supporting legs – these fasten onto a base, which provides a support for the drawing paper

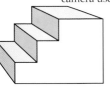
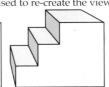

DEMONSTRATION DRAWINGS *above*
Wheatstone used these two simple drawings to explain stereoscopic vision (see caption, right). If you take an index card and place it on its end between the two pictures, you can experience the stereoscopic effect for yourself. Place your nose against the top of the card, and look at the left-hand image with your left eye and the right-hand image with your right eye. Now look with both eyes – the two images suddenly fuse and project in three dimensions from the page.

CHARLES WHEATSTONE'S STEREOSCOPE
Wheatstone first described the Stereoscope in the 1830s. His device is based on the fact that each eye focuses on an object from a slightly different angle, resulting in two slightly dissimilar images that are fused by the brain. This disparity gives us our perception of depth. Wheatstone simulated this effect by presenting each eye with images relating specifically to it. He arranged two different photographs – taken from the focus point of each eye – either side of twin mirrors angled at 45 degrees. The two images are reflected, one into each eye, by these mirrors. The images then merge to give the viewer a single image of extraordinary depth.

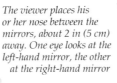

The viewer places his or her nose between the mirrors, about 2 in (5 cm) away. One eye looks at the left-hand mirror, the other at the right-hand mirror

PHOTOGRAPHY
Wheatstone took advantage of the invention of photography (1839) to show how realistic stereoscopic images could be.

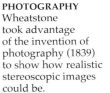

The mounts for the stereoscopic photographs can be moved backward and forward along slots so that the photographs can be positioned properly in the mirrors

Dreams of infinity

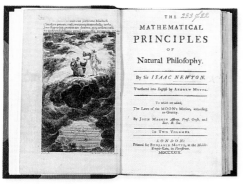

DㅜURING THE ROMANTIC PERIOD (late 18th/early 19th century), the calm, mathematically controlled space of the Renaissance – which had enjoyed a recent revival – was transformed by a new emphasis on the artist's imagination. The poet and painter William Blake (1757–1827) was among the first to rebel against the limiting role of mathematics and science, seeing these disciplines as the enemies of religious and poetic inspiration. The artist, he wrote, "who sees the infinite in all things, sees God. He who sees the Ratio only, sees himself only." Blake was not interested in elaborate spatial settings, but his dreams of infinity were shared by two masters of space and light – J.M.W. Turner (1775–1851) and John Martin (1789–1854). Their personal visions of the overwhelming power of nature were fueled by the natural sciences and perspective: John Martin even described his lofty compositions as "perspectives of feeling."

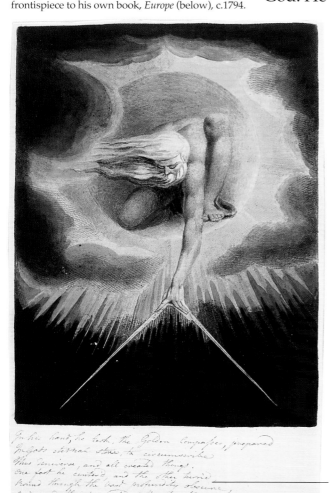

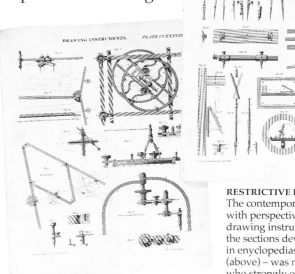

mathematics. In his own works, he left space undefined so that it didn't interfere with the clarity of his figure compositions. He also believed that life drawing – which, like perspective, was central to an artist's academic training (below) – killed the imagination. One of his guiding principles was: "Genius begins where rules end."

Blake's hand-written extract from Milton's poem Paradise Lost *refers to God's "Golden Compasses"*

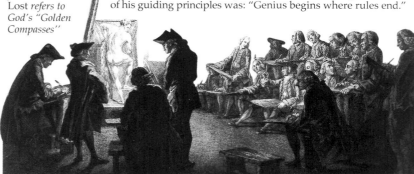

The Ancient of Days

WILLIAM BLAKE *c.1794; frontispiece of* Europe, a Prophecy; *metal-cut print, with watercolor added*
Blake used this image for the frontispiece of his prophetic poem *Europe*. It shows the God of the Old Testament in the guise of Urizen (a character invented by Blake), whom he saw as the spirit of uninspired reason. He is seen "binding the infinite" with a compass – a negative symbol of artistic, as well as biblical, creation.

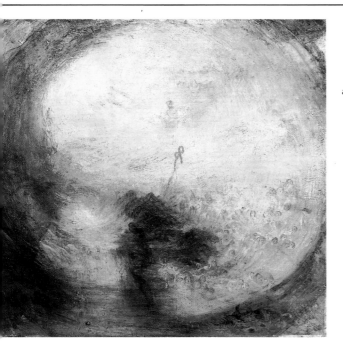

LIGHT AND COLOR – THE MORNING AFTER THE DELUGE
J.M.W. Turner; 1843; 31 x 31 in (79 x 79 cm); oil on canvas
This is a striking example of one of Turner's favorite types of spatial compositions – the vortex. The whirling mass of vibrant color seems to suck human life into "infinitude," as Turner called it, totally overwhelming the viewer with the elemental forces of water and air, expressed through light. The effect was probably inspired by illusionistic paintings on ceiling domes, as well as by the abstract power of nature.

TURNER – PROFESSOR OF PERSPECTIVE
As Professor of Perspective at the Royal Academy (1807–1828), the landscape painter Turner taught and illustrated its principles (right), highlighting the role of reflections and atmospheric color and light (pp. 28–29). Admitting that the rules of perspective were "turgid," he believed it to be useful for expressing "amplitude, quantity, and space."

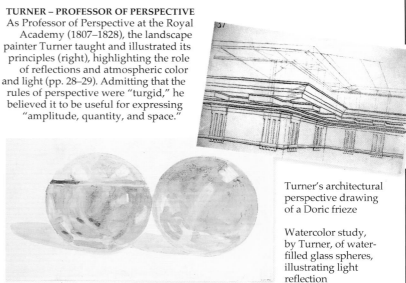

Turner's architectural perspective drawing of a Doric frieze

Watercolor study, by Turner, of water-filled glass spheres, illustrating light reflection

The Plains of Heaven

JOHN MARTIN *1833; 6 ft 6 in x 10 ft 1 in (1.98 x 3.07 m); oil on canvas*
Martin used his conventional perspective training to construct imaginary landscapes on an epic scale. His combination of vivid color and spectacular perspective vistas prompted one critic to write: "Mr. Martin must have been born with prisms for eyes." His awe-inspiring creations proved extraordinarily popular. He "ravished the senses of the multitude," declared his obituary, "and sometimes dazzled the imaginations of calmer men."

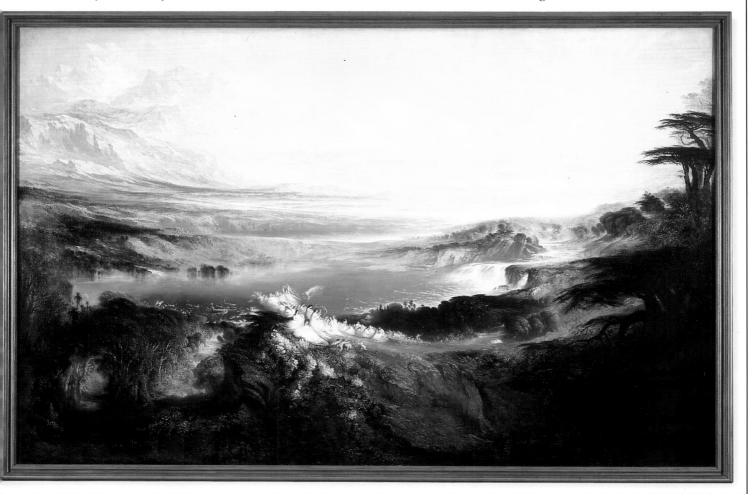

East meets West

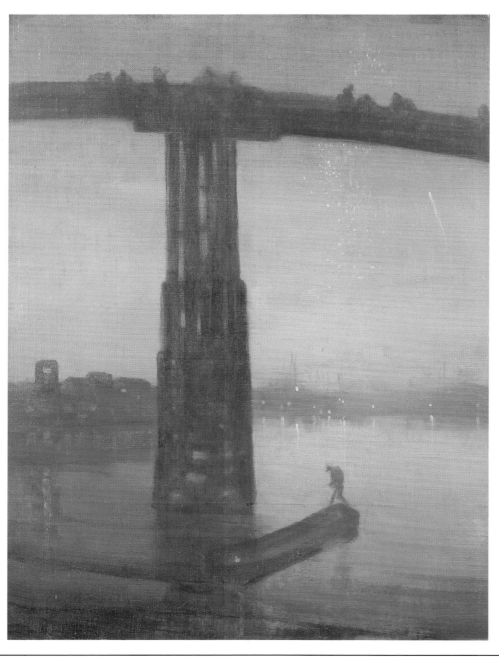

JAPANESE SIGNATURE
To emphasize his affinity with Japanese art, Whistler signed his paintings with his famous butterfly signature – in Japan, the butterfly is the symbol of the soul.

IN THE MID-19TH CENTURY, the meeting of two very different cultures gave rise to a new, refreshing approach to spatial composition. On March 31, 1854, the ports of Japan were officially opened to Western traders, paving the way for a flood of Japanese artifacts into the West, and for Japan's spectacular contributions to the International Exhibitions of 1862 (London), and 1876, 1878, and 1889 (Paris). What excited Westerners about artists such as Hokusai and Hiroshige was their use of bold "cutoff" foreground objects, astonishing viewpoints, and the interweaving of blank space with decorative forms. But the influence didn't just travel one way. The arrival of foreign traders in Japan allowed the Japanese to assimilate Western forms and themes, so that their work struck a familiar chord with Western viewers.

NOCTURNE IN BLUE AND GOLD
James Abbott McNeill Whistler
c.1872–75; 26¾ x 20 in (68 x 51 cm); oil on canvas
Anglo-American artist Whistler (1834–1903) bought some Japanese prints in Paris in 1862, which he "delighted in." *Nocturne* was inspired by Hiroshige's print of Kyo Bridge (below). The looming bulk of Battersea Bridge breaks up the space into simple portions. A small diagonal boat counterbalances the vertical of the pier, leading the eye, parallel with the bank, toward a boundless vista of still water and evening sky.

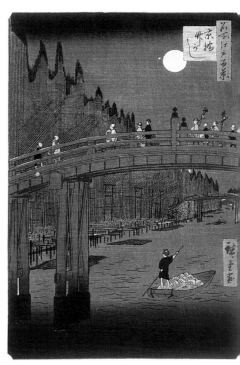

KYO-BASHI BRIDGE AND TAKE-GASHI
Ando Hiroshige; c.1857; 14 x 9½ in
(35.5 x 24 cm); colored woodblock print
Although influenced by the poetic landscapes of Katsushika Hokusai (1760–1849), Hiroshige (1797–1858) expressed the Japanese vision of landscape in a more accessible way. The arching bridge, spanning the picture width, provides a gateway to the river landscape. Floating rafts act as visual stepping stones to the echoing bridges in the distance.

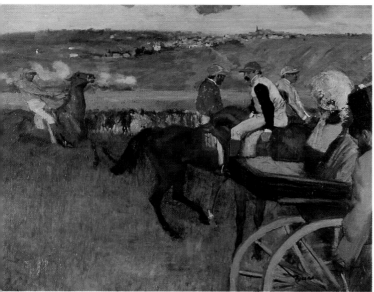

RACE COURSE *left*
Edgar Degas; 1876–87
26 x 32 in (66 x 81 cm); oil on canvas
In 1880, a critic described how the French artist Degas (1834–1917) cut off forms "as in some Japanese prints." His *Race Course* – probably inspired by Hiroshige's *Cartwheel* (right) – places the cutoff object in an extreme corner. This invites the eye to settle on a half-glimpsed foreground object and then leap into the distance. Degas owned some Hiroshige prints and was also fascinated by the way in which the recently invented "instantaneous" photograph unexpectedly cut off figures and objects.

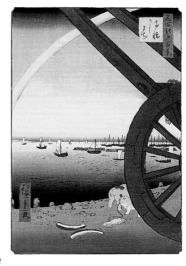

CARTWHEEL AT THE SEASHORE
Ando Hiroshige; c.1857; 14½ x 10 in (37 x 25 cm); colored woodblock print
This is a startling cutoff image that contradicts all the traditional Western ideas about central focus and compositional symmetry. The extreme close-up view and low viewpoint give viewers the impression of experiencing the scene directly. Viewers can even peep through the spokes of the giant wheel before exploring the expanse of sea and sand. Hiroshige, like Degas, may also have been influenced by photography – there is a certain snapshot immediacy, as if the wheel has just rolled into "frame."

VERTICAL PERSPECTIVE
Japanese folding screens showed Western painters that art could be ornamental and suggest space at the same time. An illusion of distance is created on the tall, narrow panels through "vertical perspective" – the farther away an object is, the higher up it is shown. On this six-paneled 18th-century screen, horizontal bands of landscape, interspersed with areas of gold leaf, set up a pattern that defines space and also acts as surface decoration.

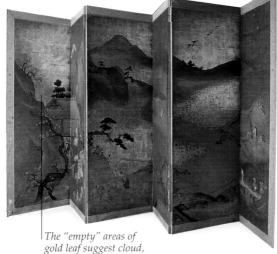

The "empty" areas of gold leaf suggest cloud, mist, or sky

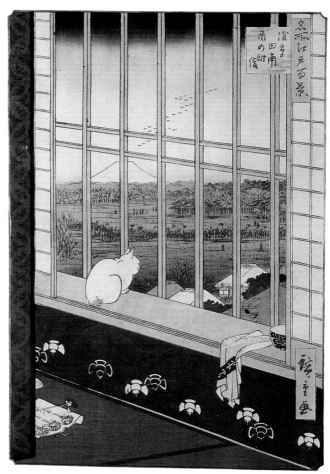

POPLARS ON THE EPTE
Claude Monet; 1891; 36½ x 29 in (92.5 x 74 cm); oil on canvas
Impressionist Claude Monet (1840–1926) responded to the simple, yet effective, way the Japanese structured space. In their prints, space is just as important as solid forms, so compositions become a "dialogue" between the two. Here, Monet used tree trunks in the same way Japanese masters often featured the uprights of their traditional window grilles (see right). The result is a subtle interplay between the surface pattern of the grillelike wall of trees and the lively blue sky beyond. Through the trees, another spatial plane can be glimpsed, containing another row of poplars. Both planes are set on the diagonal – another device favored by the Japanese.

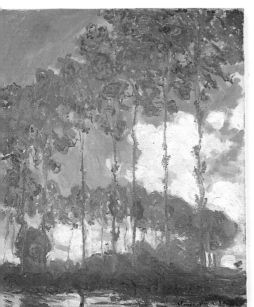

CAT LOOKING AT FIELDS AT ASAKUSA
Ando Hiroshige; c.1857; 14½ x 10 in (36.5 x 25 cm); colored woodblock print
The rigid lines of the window grille are used both to divide the interior from the outside world and to link the two. The strong grid of verticals and horizontals make the jump in scale (the cat is as big as the far mountain) seem natural. The careful perspective of the ledge on which the cat sits, and the detailed view stretching toward the horizon, show Hiroshige's interest in Western perspective techniques.

A personal perspective

Max Beckmann in 1938 – the year after he had fled Nazi Germany

> "*Space, and space again, is the infinite deity which surrounds us and in which we are ourselves contained.*"
>
> Beckmann Lecture "On My Painting" (1938)

IN THE WORKS OF the German artist Max Beckmann (1884–1950), space is the dominant means of expression. Its unique role in his art was largely determined by his World War I experiences – from which he emerged profoundly depressed and permanently scarred. At the front, he described the dark sky, lit up by exploding shells, as "an empty, indifferent, insane space." The paintings that followed his return from the war are characterized by a displaced perspective that oppresses and isolates forms and creates an overwhelming feeling of tension. Space imprisons the figures, sapping them of their energy and vitality – exposing the torment of their souls.

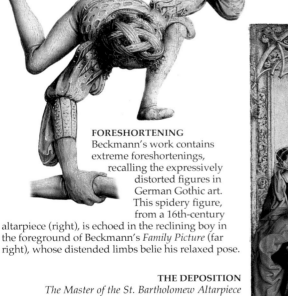

HORRORS OF WAR
As a medical orderly at the front, Beckmann pushed himself to the brink of exhaustion. He suffered a nervous breakdown and, years later, he was still haunted by nightmarish visions of dead men from the morgue. His experiences, however, only intensified his desire to "express the unutterable things in life."

Family Picture
MAX BECKMANN 1920
25½ x 39½ in (65 x 100 cm); oil on canvas
Here, a quiet, domestic scene is subtly transformed into a strangely disquieting image. Each object has its own perspective, which conflicts with the space that surrounds other forms. The room space is cramped and unstable, becoming threatening as doors, ceilings, and walls tilt inward. These inner tensions reveal the despair and anger lurking beneath the family's apparent languor.

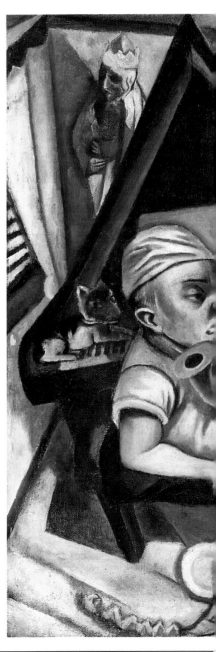

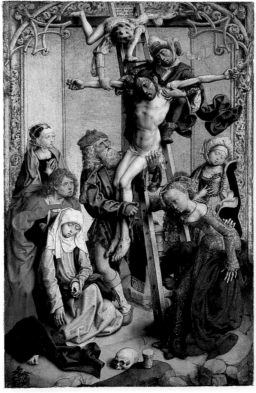

FORESHORTENING
Beckmann's work contains extreme foreshortenings, recalling the expressively distorted figures in German Gothic art. This spidery figure, from a 16th-century altarpiece (right), is echoed in the reclining boy in the foreground of Beckmann's *Family Picture* (far right), whose distended limbs belie his relaxed pose.

THE DEPOSITION
The Master of the St. Bartholomew Altarpiece
c.1500–05; 29½ x 18¾ in (75 x 47.5 cm); oil on oak
Beckmann was particularly influenced by early German works that depicted Christ's suffering. He wanted to create work "just as strong" out of the spirit of his own times. This "Deposition" (Christ being brought down from the Cross) shows the crowded shallow space, oversized figures, and strong diagonal planes that inspired him. This painting style was in turn an imitation of 15th-century sculpted tabernacles (ornamental niches).

> *"For me the metamorphosis of height, breadth and depth into the two-dimensional plane is a magical experience which gives me an inkling of that fourth dimension for which I am searching with all my soul."*

Beckmann Lecture "On My Painting" (1938)

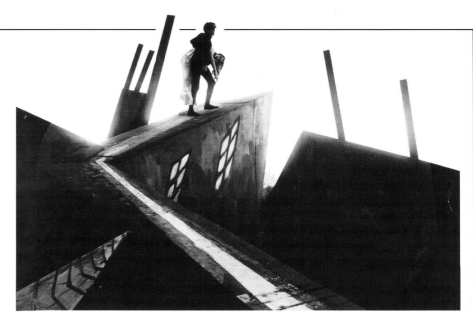

CREATING PSYCHIC SPACE

The use of space to express states of mind was also being explored by Beckmann's contemporaries. Robert Wiene's film *The Cabinet of Dr. Caligari* (1919–20) featured painted sets (by artists H. Warm, W. Reimann, and W. Rohrig) intended to reflect different psychic moods. The film, which has been described as taking place "within the dark depths of the soul," conjures up a nightmarish scenario. Its striking landscapes and architecture, constructed around oblique angles, jarring perspectives, and dangerously tilted planes, create a strange, brooding, and hostile environment.

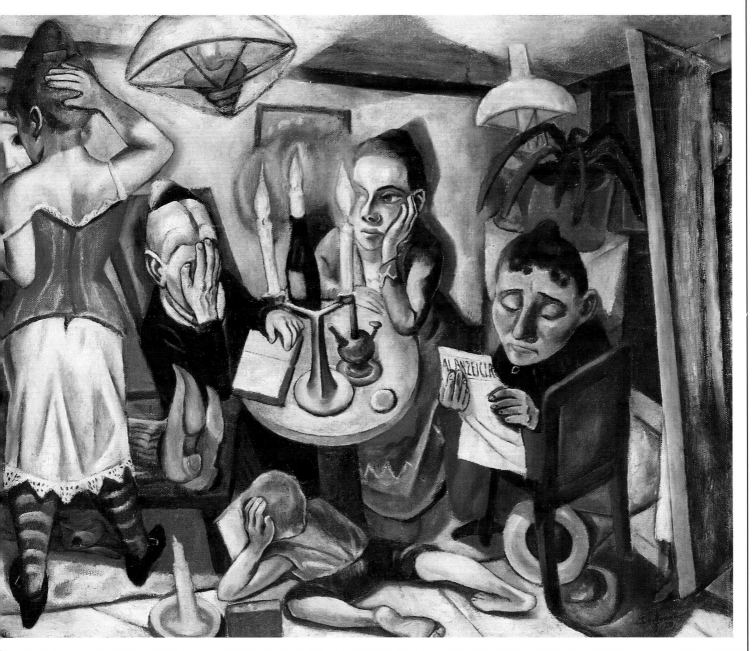

New visions of space

THE CUBIST MOVEMENT (c.1907–14) – which developed out of the inspired collaboration of Pablo Picasso and Georges Braque – set out to create a new and more convincing reality. Its revolutionary vision of space was influenced by the art of the great Post-Impressionist painter Paul Cézanne (1839–1906), who was more concerned with conveying a "feeling" of solidity and depth than with holding up a mirror to nature. This feeling was associated with the way people actually experience space – which the Cubists identified with memories of touch and movement, as well as sight. Linear perspective, dismissed by the Cubist poet Guillaume Apollinaire as a "miserable" device "for making all things shrink," was rejected in favor of a mobile perspective that splintered space into shifting geometrical planes and allowed objects to be shown from several aspects at once.

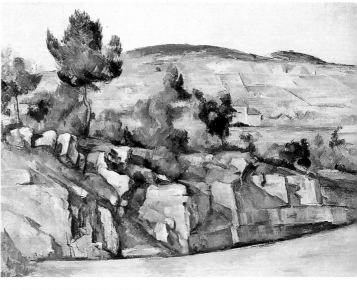

MOUNTAINS IN PROVENCE
Paul Cézanne; c.1887; 25 x 31¼ in (63.5 x 79.5 cm); oil on canvas
Cézanne's aim to create "solid and enduring" art led to a preoccupation with structure and form. In his search for permanence, instead of fleeting surface appearance, he was willing to sacrifice conventional accuracy, even breaking up and reorganizing the elements of nature in his work. In this painting, the sense of three-dimensionality is created through a geometrical arrangement of color and form, rather than conventional perspective. Paint is applied in rectangular patches and warm blocks of brown and ochre are contrasted with patches of cool gray or green.

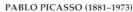
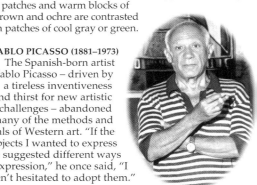

Cézanne's brushstrokes form building blocks of space and light

PABLO PICASSO (1881–1973)
The Spanish-born artist Pablo Picasso – driven by a tireless inventiveness and thirst for new artistic challenges – abandoned many of the methods and ideals of Western art. "If the subjects I wanted to express have suggested different ways of expression," he once said, "I haven't hesitated to adopt them."

Les Demoiselles d'Avignon
PABLO PICASSO
1907; 7 ft 11¼ in x 7 ft 8 in (2.43 x 2.34 m); oil on canvas
This painting, set in a brothel, shocked Picasso's friends, and transformed the direction of modern art. The figures, pushed to the front of the canvas, visually "assault" the viewer, their bodies stripped of conventional shading and perspective. Profiles sit on full-frontal heads, and spatial relationships are distorted, from the tiny still life of fruit to the monstrous nose of the squatting woman.

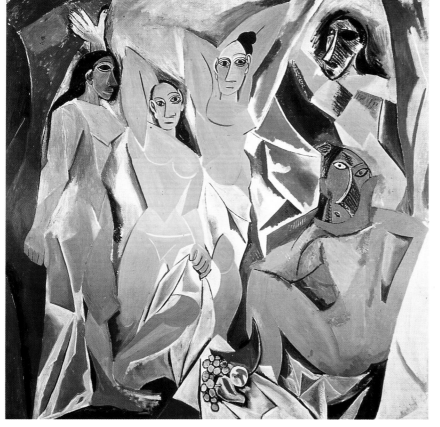

AFRICAN INSPIRATION
Picasso was influenced by the force and simplicity of African masks. He repainted the heads of the two women on the right after seeing examples of African sculpture.

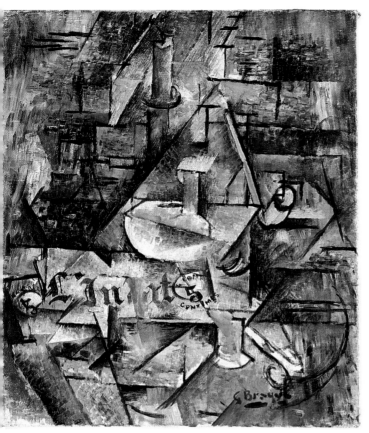

Candlestick

GEORGES BRAQUE *1911; 18 x 15 in (46 x 38 cm); oil on canvas*
This intricate still life belongs to the phase of Cubism that Braque and Picasso described as "analytical." The elements of the picture – bedside table, candle, scissors, pipe, newspaper, and their surrounding space – have been carefully analyzed, fragmented, and then reassembled. The space consists of planes faceted like diamonds and shaded so that they appear to lie at various angles to the viewer.

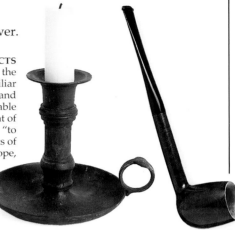

IDENTIFIABLE OBJECTS
The Cubists kept a link with the real world by including familiar objects, like this candlestick and pipe. This idea of recognizable reality led to the development of collage (from the French "to glue"), in which fragments of real objects – newspaper, rope, and so on – were stuck to the canvas. This violated, once and for all, the idea of the picture surface as a transparent plane.

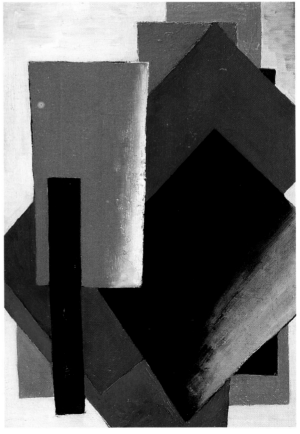

COLOR AND SPACE
Popova uses the relationship between colors to imply space. The bright red forces its way to the front of the picture, while black "sits back."

Highlighted areas (here, and on the black square) add texture, drama, and ambiguity: is this bright red shape a rectangle or a cylinder?

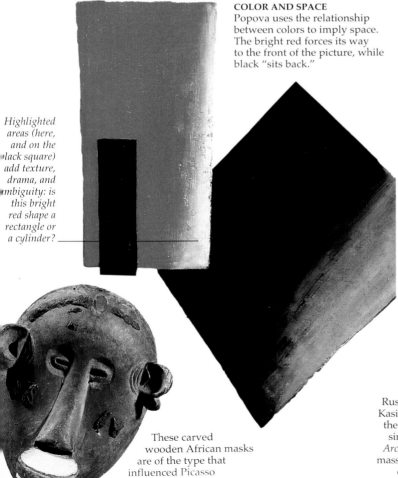

These carved wooden African masks are of the type that influenced Picasso

PICTORIAL ARCHITECTONIC
Lyubov Popova; 1916; 23½ x 15½ in (59.5 x 39.5 cm); oil on board
Russian artist Popova (1889–1924) – following in the wake of her compatriot Kasimir Malevich – took the step from Cubism to Abstraction. In Abstract art, the representation of the real world is abandoned in favor of a "pure" art of simplified forms – like the square, circle, and rectangle. Popova's *Pictorial Architectonic* builds an abstract "architecture" that, like real architecture, has mass, weight, and distance. The sensation of depth is created through strongly contrasting colors and the rhythmic overlapping of forms and planes.

Into the future

ITALIAN FUTURISM was an early 20th-century artistic movement that set out to free art from a "fossilized" past and catapult it into the modern era. Amid blazing publicity, the Futurists heralded a new form of beauty – "speed" – which evoked the new age of violence, war, communications, and technology. Aggression and destruction were paramount and, in the works of Futurism's principal artist, Umberto Boccioni (1882–1916), resulted in the violent disintegration of the picture space. The static perspective of the past was replaced by a "universal dynamism," in which motion and sensation are represented by objects and figures merging with space. In Boccioni's hands, sculpture as well as painting was used to express these ideas.

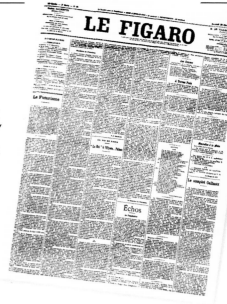

THE FUTURISTS
The leading lights of Futurism, photographed in Paris in 1912. From left to right: Russolo, Carrà, Marinetti, Boccioni, and Severini.

THE BIRTH OF FUTURISM
In a brazen piece of advertising, the poet Marinetti placed Futurism's founding *Manifesto* on the front page of *Le Figaro* (February 20, 1909). Its stirring glorification of youth and modernity persuaded the ambitious Boccioni to "enlist."

BEAUTY'S NEW FORM
In his *Manifesto*, Filippo Marinetti scorned Italy's reverence for classical art: "A racing car, its hood adorned with pipes like serpents with explosive breath ... a racing car which seem to run on gunpowder is more beautiful than the *Victory of Samothrace*" (below). His dismissal of classical beauty implied a complete rejection of Renaissance art and values.

Marinetti in his car, c.1908

Victory of Samothrace

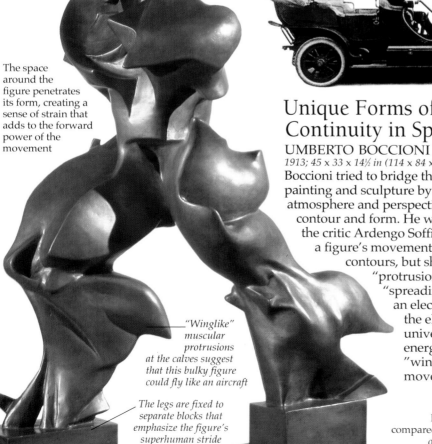

The space around the figure penetrates its form, creating a sense of strain that adds to the forward power of the movement

"Winglike" muscular protrusions at the calves suggest that this bulky figure could fly like an aircraft

The legs are fixed to separate blocks that emphasize the figure's superhuman stride

Unique Forms of Continuity in Space
UMBERTO BOCCIONI
1913; 45 x 33 x 14½ in (114 x 84 x 37 cm); bronze

Boccioni tried to bridge the gap between painting and sculpture by embracing atmosphere and perspective as well as contour and form. He was influenced by the critic Ardengo Soffici, who suggested that a figure's movements should not stop at its contours, but should be expressed through "protrusions" that impel it into space, "spreading out into infinity the way an electric wave flies out to rejoin the elemental forces of the universe." In Boccioni's figure, energy emanates in the form of "wings" that powerfully imply movement through space.

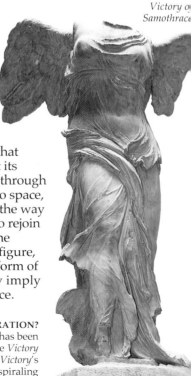

CLASSICAL INSPIRATION?
Ironically, *Unique Forms* has been compared with the classical statue *Victory of Samothrace* (right). The *Victory's* outwardly thrust wings, spiraling draperies, and forward movement set up a similar "field of force."

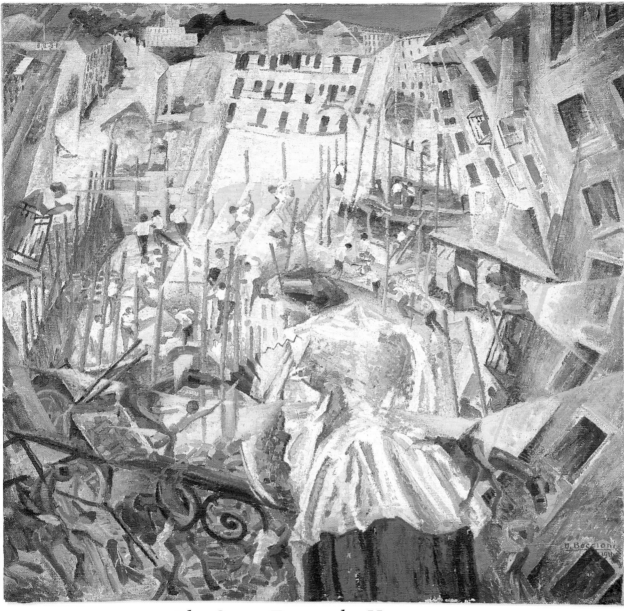

"*We declare that the whole visible world must fall in upon us...*"

Boccioni,
*Technical Manifesto
of Futurist
Sculpture* (1912)

FRAGMENTED PLANES
The buildings are the focus of the disruption of space: they display what Boccioni called "the battle of the planes."

ONLOOKERS
The rejection of a "one-eyed" perspective is suggested by the number of women leaning over balconies (front, left, and side) – all experiencing different viewpoints.

SPATIAL PUN
The horse emerging from the woman's hip may echo an idea in the Futurists' 1910 *Technical Manifesto*: "How often have we seen upon the cheek of the person with whom we are talking the horse which passes at the end of the street?" This refers to the way sight and experience merge everything together.

The Street Enters the House

UMBERTO BOCCIONI *1911*
27½ x 29½ in (70 x 75 cm); oil on canvas
In this tumultuous vision, the Renaissance idea of a painting as a view through a window is wrenched inside out. Here, the window of the canvas is thrown wide open and "all life and the noises of the street rush in at the same time as the movement and the reality of the objects outside" (Boccioni). The spectator is invaded by a clash of forms and color, creating a sensation of noise and vitality.

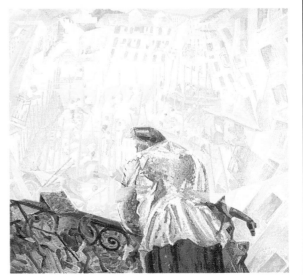

THE MOVING IMAGE
Boccioni was influenced by Futurist photographer Bragaglia, who used long exposures, during which his subject performed a simple movement. He felt that the space through which the subject moved was filled with his "soul," and aimed "to capture the form that expresses its continuity in space."

MULTIPLE VIEWPOINTS
Once he has flung open the window, Boccioni pushes the viewer out to join the woman on the balcony. He wrote: "The painter does not limit himself to what he sees in the square frame of the window, as would a mere photographer, but he also reproduces what he would see by looking out on every side from the balcony."

Subtle deception

THE ITALIAN PAINTER Giorgio de Chirico (1888–1978), while being credited with the modern revival of 15th-century perspective, deliberately undermined its qualities of logic, stability, and order. Like his Swiss contemporary Paul Klee (1879–1940), de Chirico isolated perspective horizontals, verticals, and orthogonals from their surroundings so that they almost become haunting arrangements of lines. Viewers interpreting these lines as indicators of distance and depth find themselves strangely disoriented (in de Chirico) or gently deceived (in Klee).

A DEHUMANIZED ENVIRONMENT
De Chirico's impersonal use of perspective, in which the human viewpoint loses its central role, is embodied by the faceless mannequins – a combination of tailor's dummy and artist's anatomical model (above) – that "people" his works.

Set squares similar to those shown on Klee's easel (oval picture on opposite page)

The Disquieting Muses
GIORGIO DE CHIRICO 1916–17
37 x 24½in (94 x 62 cm); tempera on cardboard

The disquieting effect of de Chirico's *Muses* (in mythology, beings who inspired creativity) comes largely from the irrational perspective and the unnatural light. The orthogonals of the boarded floor slope so steeply that the ground – rather than calmly receding, as in Van Eyck's "*Arnolfini Marriage*" (p. 11) – seems to tilt upward like a drawbridge. Viewers trying to follow these orthogonals toward the background buildings could find themselves either toppling over the mock horizon or getting lost in the solid blocks of shadow, which have an existence of their own.

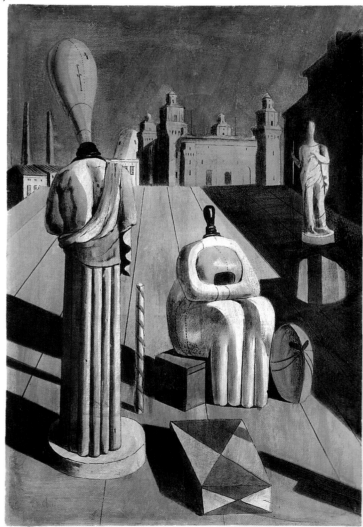

GROUND LEVEL
The floor projects over the bases of the buildings, leaving the viewer unsure about where the ground actually begins.

SPACE AND TIME
If the lines of the three-dimensional architecture in the background are logically extended, it is clear that the buildings bear little relation to each other. They are locked in their own space and time, like the architectural figures and forms in the foreground.

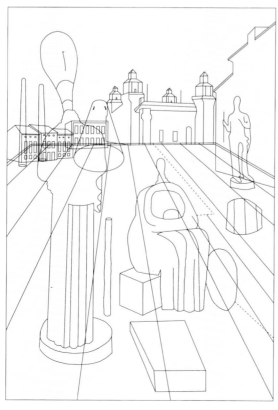

INDIVIDUAL PERSPECTIVES *left*
The conflicting styles and cultures that de Chirico alludes to in this painting – classical statues, Renaissance buildings, and 20th-century factory chimneys – are echoed in the collision of multiple viewpoints. Each object has its own perspective and scale that isolate it from the others and give it a mysterious life of its own. When viewed together, the illogical nature of the perspective creates an eerie feeling of timelessness and dislocation. The Italian square reverberates with the ghosts of its past, and viewers are reminded of their own solitude.

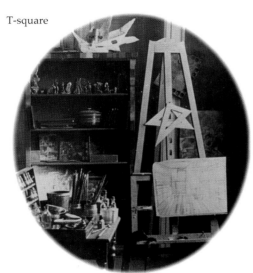

PRECISION TOOLS

Technical drawing tools – like the triangle (or set-square) and the T-square – were used by de Chirico and Klee for drawing perspective lines. De Chirico even included these devices in his paintings – in several of his compositions, luridly lit set-squares, rules, compasses, and frames are stacked on top of one another to create complex interlocking shapes with tantalizing glimpses of space in between.

T-square

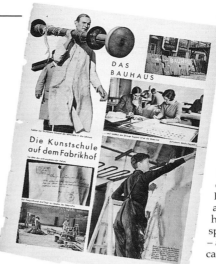

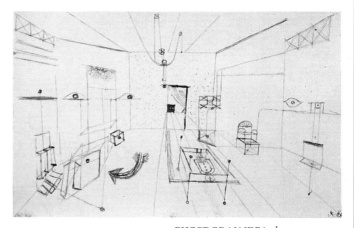

KLEE'S BAUHAUS TEACHING

In January 1921, Klee joined the teaching staff at Walter Gropius's newly founded Bauhaus – the Weimar school of architecture and applied arts that had such an impact on European industrial design. As part of his duties, Klee delivered a lecture on perspective on November 28, 1921, choosing to demonstrate to his students the deceptive qualities of perspective space. He explained to them that what appears to be logical doesn't have to be interpreted logically. A spatial illusion is always imaginary – and a surface subdivided by lines can mean many things.

WORK IN PROGRESS

Klee began to experiment with perspective images around 1920. The start of a perspective interior can be seen on his easel (above), together with the set-squares he would have used to rule the lines. In his finished works (below), he kept a basic framework, adding subtle color. To him, lines described a mood and fantasy, as well as conveying space and objects.

GHOST OF AN IDEA *above*
Klee's drawings were his greatest source of inspiration. This ink sketch, on which he wrote the title *Perspective-Spuk* (*Phantom Perspective*), forms the basis of the painting of the same name (left). He used paper painted with wet black oil as a "carbon," tracing the image's outline with a stylus onto a second sheet.

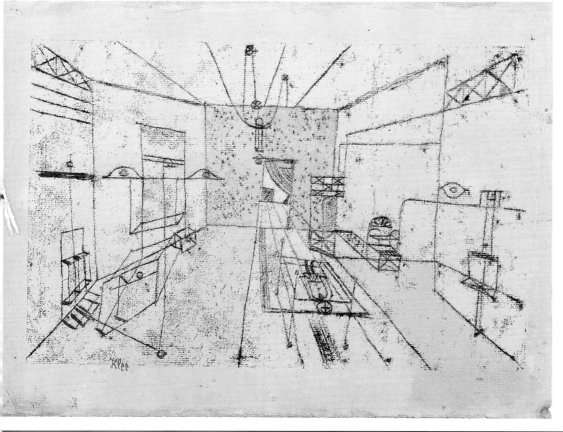

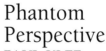

Phantom Perspective

PAUL KLEE *1920*

9½ x 12 in (24 x 30.5 cm); watercolor and transferred printing ink on paper

In the 1920s, Klee produced several ghostly interiors with transparent furniture and radiating perspective lines. The furniture seems three-dimensional, but the person in the center is compressed into a pair of flat rectangles. With its multiple walls and watchful eyes, the room has been interpreted as a bizarre laboratory or gymnasium. The perspective can be seen as both a fanciful space and a psychological play of lines.

Ambiguous space

THE SURREALISTS Salvador Dali (1904–1989) and René Magritte (1898–1967) explored the world of dreams and the subconscious through totally traditional techniques – Dali even described his paintings as "hand-painted photographs." Using conventional perspective, they lured viewers into a mirror-image world and then confronted them with absurd or puzzling images. Caught off-guard and stripped of their common sense, spectators are forced to question their powers of perception – if things are not as we see them, then how can they be represented as they really are? Such ambiguities were explored by the Dutch graphic artist M.C. Escher (1898–1972) and the American Adelbert Ames, Jr. (1880–1955). Their works show that perspective illusion relies, for its effect, on the viewer's expectations – and these are easily confused!

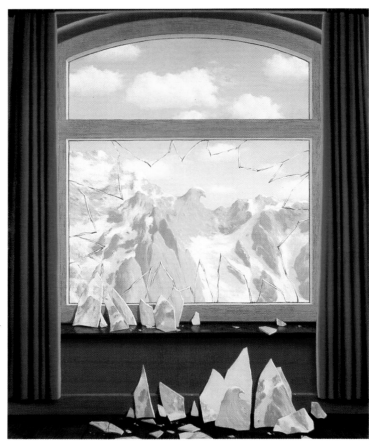

THE DOMAIN OF ARNHEIM
René Magritte; 1949; 39 x 32 in (99.5 x 81.5 cm); oil on canvas
Magritte presents the idea of a painting as a view through a window as an enigma. In *Arnheim*, the "window" of the canvas and the painted window look out onto an eagle-shaped mountain. The shattered window has left landscape fragments on the floor – and we realize that the glass can't be transparent.

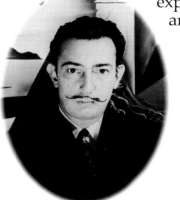

DALI'S DREAM IMAGES
Dali used traditional perspective to describe the workings of the mind. Here he poses in front of the dream sequences he designed for Alfred Hitchcock's film *Spellbound* (1945).

The Persistence of Memory

SALVADOR DALI *1931*
9½ x 13 in (24 x 33 cm); oil on canvas
The Spanish artist Dali once stated that his purpose was "to systematize confusion and thus help discredit completely the world of reality." Here, he creates an illusionistic landscape from layers of graded color, only to undermine it through a startling combination of images. The painting depicts a real Spanish beach in the glowing colors of a touched-up photograph. But the embryonic creature and the melting watches come from Dali's personal obsessions.

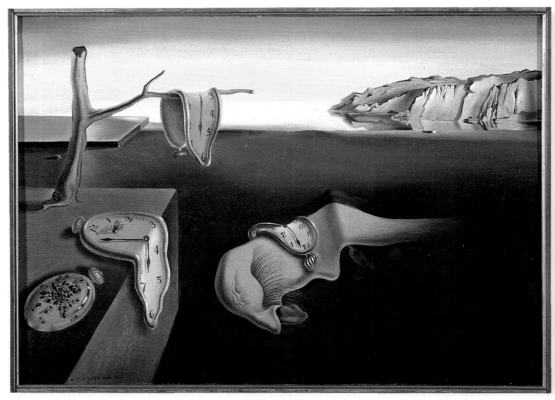

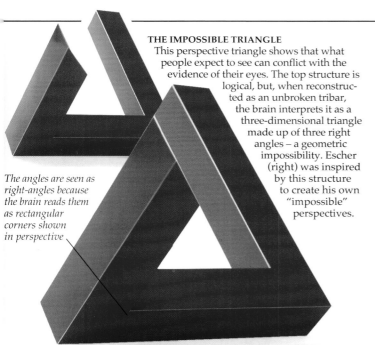

THE IMPOSSIBLE TRIANGLE

This perspective triangle shows that what people expect to see can conflict with the evidence of their eyes. The top structure is logical, but, when reconstructed as an unbroken tribar, the brain interprets it as a three-dimensional triangle made up of three right angles – a geometric impossibility. Escher (right) was inspired by this structure to create his own "impossible" perspectives.

The angles are seen as right-angles because the brain reads them as rectangular corners shown in perspective

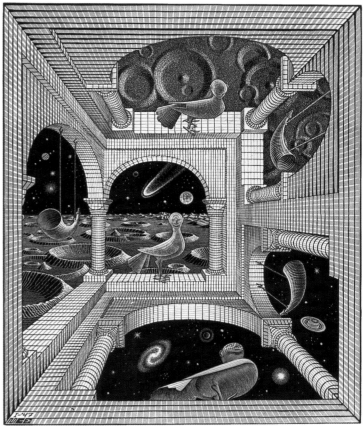

PERSPECTIVE FANTASIES *left*

The Surrealists admired a series of fantastic imaginary prisons (c.1745 & 1760) that were produced by the 18th-century etcher G.B. Piranesi. These huge dungeons, with their overpowering perspective, have been compared to the hallucinations of opium dreams. Spiral staircases and walkways lead nowhere, windows look onto the inside as well as the outside, and drawbridges open onto a giant void. Piranesi produced this series at such speed that it is unlikely that the spatial ambiguities were intentional.

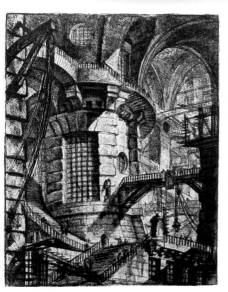

Other World

M.C. ESCHER *1947; 12½ x 10¼ in (32 x 26 cm); colored wood engraving*
This print is not what it seems. The familiar illusionistic architecture makes us think that we can decipher the space of the picture, but, as we explore each of the views, we realize that we have stepped into an impossible world. The architecture, lunar landscape, and objects are shown from three contradictory viewpoints, so that terms like floor, wall, and ceiling lose their relevance. All the views, however, lead conventionally to the same central vanishing point.

THE AMES ROOM

This room was devised by the artist Adelbert Ames, Jr., to show just how deceptive the geometry of three-dimensional objects can be. We think that we see a rectangular room inhabited by two abnormal people; but the room is not rectangular, and its planes – walls, floor, and ceiling – are not set at right angles to one another. It is actually a six-sided irregular construction with sloping floor, ceiling, and rear wall, inhabited by people of normal size.

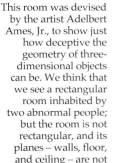

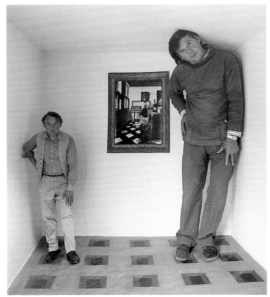

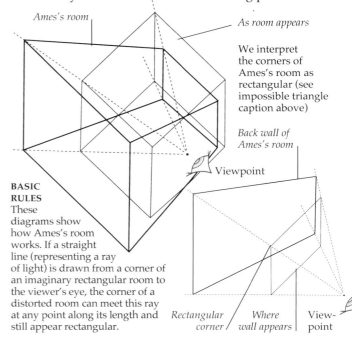

Ames's room

As room appears

We interpret the corners of Ames's room as rectangular (see impossible triangle caption above)

Back wall of Ames's room

Viewpoint

BASIC RULES

These diagrams show how Ames's room works. If a straight line (representing a ray of light) is drawn from a corner of an imaginary rectangular room to the viewer's eye, the corner of a distorted room can meet this ray at any point along its length and still appear rectangular.

Rectangular corner / *Where wall appears* | *View-point*

Popular perspective

BY THE 1960s, perspective images had been so thoroughly exploited by the mass media – film, photography, comics, and advertising – that they had become part of the popular vocabulary. Perspective was again recognized as one of the most powerful tools of communication, bringing clarity and directness to the visual message. This perspective was different from that of the Renaissance – it was witty, banal, even brash, echoing the fast-changing values of a consumer-led society. Pop artists Richard Hamilton (b.1922) and Roy Lichtenstein (b.1923) used perspective to frame their responses to modern experience. The images are radical, but their compositions sit comfortably within the continuing perspective tradition.

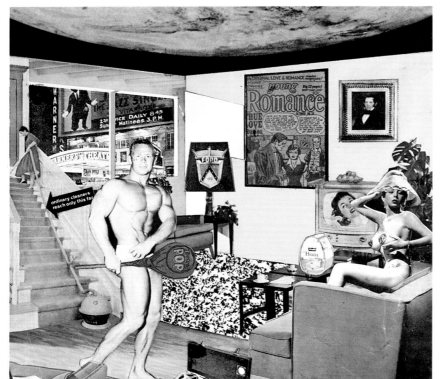

Just what is it that makes today's homes so different, so appealing?

RICHARD HAMILTON
1956; 10¼ x 9¾ in (26 x 25 cm); collage on paper
Hamilton's satirical collage displays modern life and aspirations within a traditional perspective setting. The conventional room space stresses parallels between past and present – as does the juxtaposition of an ancestral portrait with a framed *Young Romance* cover. Stairs, seen through the exaggerated perspective of the camera lens, are shown primarily to emphasize the reach of the vacuum cleaner!

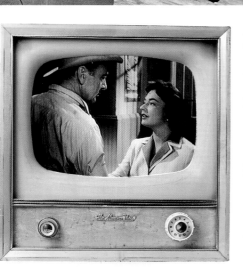

THE SCREEN IMAGE
Television is one of pop art's favorite motifs – as a symbol of modern culture, and also because of the extra dimension it can give to a picture. Artists use it rather as they would a view through a window: to represent another vista – of space, light, sound, and movement. Television screen images also transform reality, forcing viewers to look at the world in new ways. One pop art commentator wrote: "The movie close-up, black and white, technicolor and wide screen, the billboard extravaganzas, and finally, the introduction through television, of this blatant appeal to our eye into the home ... has made available an imagery so pervasive, persistent and compulsive that it had to be noticed."

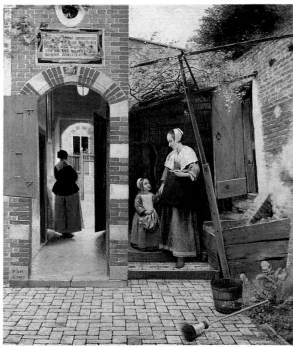

THE COURTYARD OF A HOUSE IN DELFT
Pieter de Hooch; 1685; 29 x 23½ in (73.5 x 60 cm); oil on canvas
Hamilton's interior, with its spatial "compartments," resembles the arrangement of Dutch 17th-century scenes – even providing a glimpse of the outside world beyond. The solid, domestic values of *The Courtyard*, however, are a far cry from Hamilton's world of glamour and material seduction.

Blam

ROY LICHTENSTEIN

1962; 5 ft 7 in x 6 ft 7 in (1.70 x 2.0 m); oil on canvas

Lichtenstein borrowed the methods of comic strips to show how easily people's emotions can be manipulated. Although the picture space is flattened, perspective is still *Blam*'s most expressive element.

Dramatic foreshortening and a close viewpoint make the airplane look as if it is bursting out of the picture space. The artist remains detached by virtue of his mechanical dot technique, painted to imitate cheap printing processes.

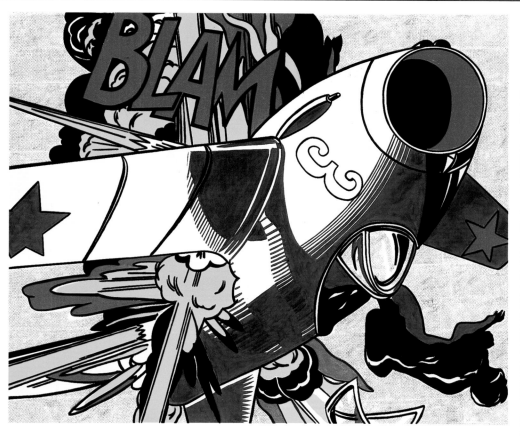

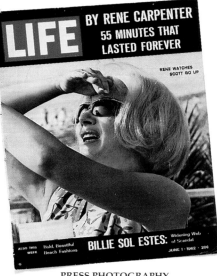

PRESS PHOTOGRAPHY

The popular press, in particular *Life* magazine, exerted a major influence on pop art. This 1962 cover shows how *Life*'s photographers achieved immediacy through adventurous camera angles and unusual framing of the image. Some artists incorporated *Life* covers directly into their work.

ADVERTISING TECHNIQUES *right*
The hypnotic power of perspective has been recognized for a long time – Andrea Mantegna's *Dead Christ* (p. 21) is so skillfully foreshortened that the body seems to follow the viewer, forcing anyone looking at the painting to concentrate on its religious message. Early on, advertisers discovered that they could exploit this phenomenon – using exaggerated perspective to propel their images out of the picture space and grab the viewer's attention. This British World War I recruiting poster shows Lord Kitchener's sharply foreshortened arm and pointing finger arresting passersby in their tracks.

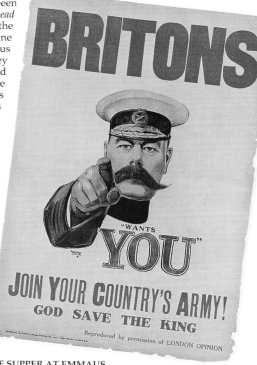

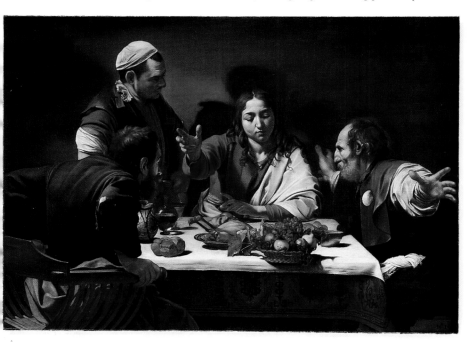

THE SUPPER AT EMMAUS

Caravaggio; c.1596–1602
4 ft 7½ in x 6 ft 5 in (1.41 x 1.96 m); oil on canvas
Blam uses the same close-up perspective as *The Supper at Emmaus*. The background is flat and in deep shadow, forcing the viewer to focus on dramatically lit forms, which spring out of the darkness. Caravaggio shows the moment when the resurrected Christ is recognized by his apostles. One throws his arms apart so violently that his hand seems to puncture the picture surface.

Glossary

Anamorphosis An image that has been distorted – so that it appears stretched – by using an extreme case of normal perspective procedure. When viewed from a specific point, or as a reflection in a curved mirror, the image returns to normal (p. 32).

Braccio (plural, "braccia") A unit of measurement, used in Renaissance Italy, of about 23 in (57 cm). It was based on the length of an arm (*braccio* is Italian for "arm"). Alberti scaled his perspective system according to the height of a man three braccia tall.

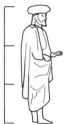

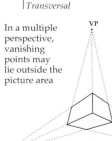

Alberti based his system on a man three braccia tall

Centric point/ centric ray The centric point is the point at the center of a perspective image, opposite the viewpoint. The centric ray is an imaginary ray of light joining the centric point to the viewpoint. The distance between these two points

is the viewing distance. In a one-point perspective, the centric point coincides with the vanishing point.

Checkback line A line drawn diagonally through the squares in a "perspective pavement," to check the construction's accuracy (pp. 13, 22).

Distance points The two points on the horizon line, to left and right, where diagonals through the tiles of a "perspective pavement" converge. They are usually outside the picture space and are the same distance from the vanishing point as the viewpoint is from the picture plane.

Field of vision The area of vision that can be taken in by the eye, or covered by a perspective picture. The former is about 90° on either side of the centric ray. The latter is smaller, often said to be about 30° on either side of the centric ray.

Foreshortening The method by which the intervals of a "perspective pavement" or the parts of an object are diminished so that they appear shorter and narrower as they recede.

Ground plane The plane stretching from the bottom edge of the picture

plane to the horizon. It also forms the "ground" on which the viewer stands.

Horizon line This line represents the line in nature where earth and sky appear to meet. In perspective, the horizon is an imaginary line drawn across the picture plane at the viewer's eye level.

Multiple vanishing points A regular-shaped object has more than one vanishing point when it is not parallel with or perpendicular to the picture plane. For example, if it is tilted at 45° to the picture plane, the lines of its sides converge to two vanishing points on the horizon line. If its planes are tilted up or down, there is a third vanishing point above or below.

Orthogonals Diagonal lines drawn from the subdivided base line of the picture plane to the vanishing point. They represent receding parallels (perpendicular to the picture plane) and draw the viewer's eye into depth.

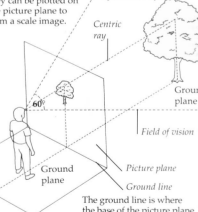

Orthogonals and transversals are clearly defined in this "perspective pavement" by Lorenzetti

Picture plane The flat surface on which a picture is painted. This vertical plane is imagined as a windowpane between the viewer (or artist) and the scene depicted in the picture.

Transversals The horizontal lines of a "perspective pavement."

Vanishing point The point on the horizon that represents the far distance. In one-point perspectives, it is the one point to which all parallel lines receding from the spectator meet in the distance. It is directly opposite the viewpoint and is therefore always at the spectator's eye level.

Viewing point The fixed viewing position from which the perspective is constructed and from where it is designed to be seen. A normal viewpoint is at head height, with the viewer standing on the ground plane. A high or low viewpoint dramatically alters a picture's perspective.

Step-by-step perspective summary

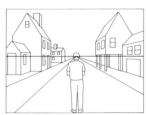

1. Normal viewpoint The eye level of the spectator is always related directly to the horizon line of the picture. When the spectator is standing on the ground plane, the horizon line is at head height.

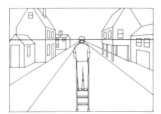

2. High viewpoint If the spectator is standing on a stepladder, looking down at the same scene, the horizon line will still be at eye level, but more of the ground plane will be visible.

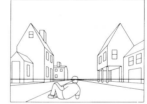

3. Low viewpoint If the spectator's viewing position is low down, the same principle applies. The horizon line will be lower down, and less of the ground plane will be visible.

4. Perspective principles The diagram below illustrates some of the basics of linear perspective. The spectator is imagined as standing on the ground plane in a fixed position, with the picture plane directly in front of him or her. This picture plane is like a large window, through which rays of light pass. As they reflect from an object to the spectator's eye, they can be plotted on the picture plane to form a scale image.

The centric ray passes from the part of the object on which the eye is focused, back to the spectator's eye

Centric ray

Ground plane

60°

Field of vision

Picture plane

Ground line

Ground plane

The ground line is where the base of the picture plane meets the ground plane

5. The vanishing point In this "ideal" one-point perspective (left), linear perspective divides the picture space into a cube, with squared pavement, walls, and ceiling. All the receding parallels (floor tiles, table top, tops and bottoms of door and window) lead to the central vanishing point (VP), located on the horizon line (HL).

Orthogonal

Transversal

In a multiple perspective, vanishing points may lie outside the picture area

Once DP is known, X can be plotted: VP to DP=VP to X

The DP on the left is not shown

6. Distance point *above right* The distance point (DP) is the point to which diagonal lines through the squares of a "perspective pavement" converge on the horizon line (HL). This point is always at 45° to the horizon. It can be used to calculate how far the viewpoint (X) is from the picture plane.

45°

X

Picture plane, from the edge

7. Three-point perspective This tilted cube has three vanishing points (VP) because it is presented at an angle to the viewer. There are two vanishing points on the horizon line (HL), and, because the cube is tilted upward, there is another vanishing point above.

VP

HL

VP.   HL   . VP

8. Foreshortening This diagram shows how the dimensions of a figure are affected by foreshortening. The unforeshortened figure is divided into units and placed sideways, with its feet at the edge of the picture plane. Where the lines drawn from the units to the vanishing point (VP, which coincides with the viewpoint) cross the edge of the picture plane, the divisions of the foreshortened figure can be drawn.

HL   VP

Featured works

Look here to find the location of, and complete details about, the works featured in the book.

Throughout the book, some works have been given their "popular" titles (these appear in the book with inverted commas). This section gives the correct catalog titles of these works. (For example, see *"The Arnolfini Marriage,"* pp. 10–11.)

This section also includes photographic acknowledgments, although more information can be found under "Acknowledgments," on p. 64.

Every effort has been made to trace the copyright holders and we apologize in advance for any unintentional omissions. We would be pleased to insert the appropriate acknowledgment in any subsequent edition of this publication.

t: top; *b*: bottom; *c*: center; *l*: left; *r*: right

Abbreviations:
BL=British Library, London; BM=The Trustees of the British Museum, London; NGL=Reproduced by courtesy of the Trustees, The National Gallery, London; TG=Tate Gallery, London; SM=Science Museum, London BAL=Bridgeman Art Library

Front Cover: *tl & tr*: Measuring instruments, BM; *cr*: From *Le Due Regole della Prospettiva Pratica*, Vignola (see p6); *br*: Surveying instrument (see p39); *cl*: *Pictorial Architectonic* (see p53); Claude Glass (see p44); *c*: *The Annunciation*, NGL (see p22) **Inside front flap:** *b*: Camera obscura (see p43) **Back Cover:** Clockwise from top right: Drawing instruments (see p32); open book, *Prospettiva Pratica*, Cigoli (see p44); Camera Lucida (see p45); *The Flood* (see p17); Zograscope (see p44)

p1 (Half Title): Oculus, Andrea Mantegna (see p20) **p2:** *tl*: Dürer woodcut (see p26); *cl*: Measuring instruments, BM; *c*: *"The Mill"* (see p44); *cr*: Claude Glass (see p44); *bl*: *The Street Enters the House* (see p55); *br*: Tent-type camera obscura (see p43) **p3 (Title Page):** *cr*: see p46; *bl*: *Poplars on the Epte* (see p49); *c*: Hoogstraten peepshow box (see p36) **p4:** *tr*: *Crucifix* (see p15); *cl*: Ancient Egyptian sketchpad (see p8); *bl*: Ancient Greek vase (see p9); *br*: portrait Prince Edward VI (see p33) **p5:** *br* (top): Dürer's *Proportions* (see p35); *br* (bottom): Vignola's *Five Orders of Architecture* (see p35)

Pages 6-7 What is perspective?
p6: *tl*: from *Le Due Regole della Prospettiva Pratica*, Jacopo Barozzi da Vignola, E. Danti, Rome, 1583 **p7:** *tl*: *St. Jerome in his Study*, Antonello da Messina, NGL; *r*: William Hogarth's *Perspectival Absurdities*, from J. Kirby's *Dr. Brook Taylor's Method of Perspective Made Easy in Both Theory and Practice*, Ipswich, 1754

Pages 8-9 Early approaches
p8: *tl*: Ancient Egyptian Sketchpad, BM; *tr*: Egyptian wall painting: *Fowling the Marshes* (from the tomb of Nebamum Thebes. c.1400 B.C.), BM; *b*: triptych: *The Virgin and Child with Saints*, Duccio, NGL **p9:** *t*: *Saint John the Baptist retiring to the Desert*, Giovanni di Paolo, NGL; *c*: Bayeux Tapestry: Harold's Oath to William, Musée de Bayeux Collection/Michael Holford; *br*: Greek vase, BM (ref: F373)

Pages 10-11 Defining space
p10: *tl*: *La Foire Lendit du Pontifical de Sens*, Manuscript (Latin 963 f. 264), Bibliothèque Nationale, Paris/BAL; *tr*: fresco from the House of Livia, Palatine Hill, Rome, 1st century A.D.; *cl*: *Herod's Feast*, Giotto, from St. John cycle in Peruzzi Chapel, Santa Croce, Florence; *br*: *The Presentation in the Temple*, Ambrogio Lorenzetti, Uffizi, Florence **p11:** *tr*: *"The Arnolfini Marriage"* – full catalog title, *The Portrait of Giovanni (?) Arnolfini and his Wife Giovanna Cenami (?)*, Jan van Eyck, NGL; *br*: *The Presentation of the Virgin*, Taddeo Gaddi, Baroncelli Chapel, Santa Croce/Scala

Pages 12-13 The "invention" of perspective
p12: *tl*: Medal of Alberti by Matteo de' Pasti, BM; **pp12-13:** *c*: *The Selling of the Host*, Paolo Uccello, Urbino, Palazzo Ducale/Scala; *bl*: detail from altarpiece: *The Martyrdom of Saint Sebastian*, Antonio and Piero Pollaiuolo, NGL; *br*: *St Anthony Healing the Young Man's Foot*, Donatello, high altar, S. Antonio, Padua/Scala **p13:** *cr*: Map IX, Ptolemaic world map, 1486/Michael Holford

Pages 14-15 A "hole in the wall"
p14: *l*: Santa Maria Novella, Florence; *r*: *The Trinity*, Masaccio, S. Maria Novella, Florence/Scala **p15:** *tl*: Interior shot of S. Maria Novella, featuring *Trinity*; *tc*: Holy Water basin, S. Maria Novella; *tr*: *Crucifix*, Master of St. Francis, NGL; *bl*: *The Trinity*/Scala

Pages 16-17 Playful perspective
p16: *t*: Drawing of chalice, Paolo Uccello, Dept. of Prints and Drawings, Uffizi, Florence/Scala **pp16-17:** *b*: *The Battle of San Romano*, Paolo Uccello, NGL **p17:** *tr*, left panel: *The Battle of San Romano*, NGL; center panel: *Michelotto da Cotignola* (also called *"The Battle of San Romano"*), Paolo Uccello, c.1440-50, Louvre, Paris; right panel: *The Unhorsing of Bernardino della Carda* (also called *"The Battle of San Romano"*), Paolo Uccello, 1450s, Uffizi, Florence/Scala; *c*: *The Flood*, Paolo Uccello, Chiostro Verde ("Green Cloister"), Santa Maria Novella, Florence

Pages 18-19 Divine measurement
p18: *tl, c*: *De Prospectiva Pingendi*, fig. LI (TAV. XXVII), (TAV. X), BL **pp18-19:** *The Flagellation*, Piero della Francesca, Galleria Nazionale, Urbino/Scala

Pages 20-21 Eyewitness art
p20: *tl*: Bust of Andrea Mantegna, on Mantegna's tomb, attrib. Andrea Mantegna, Sant' Andrea, Mantua/Scala; *tr*: *The Martyrdom of St. James*, Andrea Mantegna, Ovetari Chapel, Church of the Eremitani, Padua, BL; *b*: Oculus, from the "Painted Room" (*Camera Picta*), Andrea Mantegna, Palazzo Ducale (Gonzaga Palace), Mantua/Scala. *Camera Picta* also known as the *Camera degli Sposi* ("Bridal Chamber") **p21:** *cr*: Drawing, *Death of the Virgin*, Jacopo Bellini, BM; *tl*: *"Triptych" showing the Epiphany, Circumcision, and the Ascension (The Uffizi "Triptych")*, Andrea Mantegna, Uffizi, Florence/Scala; *b*: *The Dead Christ*, Andrea Mantegna, Brera Gallery (full name: Pinacoteca di Brera), Milan/Scala

Pages 22-23 Art for art's sake
The Annunciation, Carlo Crivelli, NGL

Pages 24-25 Leonardo's explorations
p24: *t*: Perspective section from Leonardo's *Treatise on Painting*, Bibliothèque de l'Institut, Paris/Bulloz; *cr*: preparatory drawing for *The Adoration of the Magi*, Leonardo, Dept. of Prints and Drawings, Uffizi, Florence; *bl*: *The Annunciation*, Leonardo, Uffizi, Florence **p25:** *t*: *The Last Supper*, Leonardo, Santa Maria delle Grazie, Milan/Scala; *bl*: *The Last Supper* in situ in the Refectory, Santa Maria delle Grazie, Milan/Soprintendenza per i Beni Artistici e Storici, Milano/Laboratorio Fotoradio-grafico della Soprintendenza

Pages 26-27 Dürer's perspective aids
p26: *tl*: Self-portrait, Albrecht Dürer, Louvre, Paris; *tr*: Woodcut of compass shop, 1568, Jost Amman *cl*: Woodcut from Dürer's *Treatise on Measurement (Underweysung der Messung)*, 1525; *b*: Woodcut from *Treat. on M.*, rev. ed., 1538; **p27:** *t*: Woodcut from *Treat. on M.*, 1538 ed.; *cr*: Woodcut from *Treat. on M.*, 1525 ed. *cl*: *Practical Perspective (Prospettiva Pratica)*, Cigoli, Dept. of Prints and Drawings, Uffizi, Florence; *br*: Dürer's pen, Germanisches Nationalmuseum, Nürnberg

Pages 28-29 Atmospheric perspective
p28: *tl*: Ancient Roman wall painting, originally in Pompeii, now in the Museo Nazionale, Naples/André Held; *b*: *The Virgin of the Rocks*, Leonardo, NGL **p29:** *t*: *Mountain View* (Ming period)/BAL; *cl*: Gerard David, *Canon Bernardinus de Salviatis and Three Saints*, NGL; *cr*: Turner's paintbox, TG; *b*: *Norham Castle, Sunrise*, J.M.W. Turner, TG

Pages 30-31 Room with a view
p30: *tr*: Exterior of Villa Farnesina, Rome; **pp30-31:** *c*: Salone delle Prospettive, Villa Farnesina, Rome, Baldassare Peruzzi **p31:** *tr*: "Room of the Masks," in the House of Augustus, Palatine Hill, Rome, 1st century A.D./Scala; *br*: "Comic Scene," photographed from p26, 1559-62 edition, of *Il Libro Secondo d'Architettura (Second Book of Architecture)*, Sebastiano Serlio

Pages 32-33 Hidden messages
p32: *tl*: Case of drawing instruments from the Barthelomewe Newsum (London Clockmaker) Compendium, c.1570, BM; *tr*: *The Ambassadors*, Hans Holbein, NGL **p33:** *tr*: Photograph of rectified skull, NGL; *br*: Anamorphic portrait of Prince Edward VI, William Scrots, National Portrait Gallery, London

Pages 34-35 Works of reference
pp34-35: *Las Meninas*, Diego Velázquez, © Museo del Prado, Madrid **pp34-35:** *t*: Drawing instruments from B. Newsum Compend. (see p32) **p35:** *tc*: from *Book of New Instruments of Geometry*, Andres Garcia de Cespedes, BL; *tr* (top): from Witelo's *Optics*, photographed from Alhazen's *Thesaurus of Optics*, 1572; *tr* (bottom): Frontispiece from Daniele Barbaro's *Practical Perspective* (1980 ed. of original 1569 ed.), reproduced with the kind permission of Arnaldo Forni Editore, Italy; *cr*: Frontispiece from *The New Science*, 1550, Niccolò Tartaglia; *bl* (top): Latin ed. of one of the *Four Books on Human Proportion*, 1557, Albrecht Dürer; *br* (bottom): *The Five Orders of Architecture*, 1583, Giacomo Barozzi da Vignola

Pages 36-37 Hoogstraten's peepshow
pp36-37: Full catalog title: *A Peepshow with Views of the Interior of a Dutch House*, Samuel van Hoogstraten, NGL **p37:** *tr*: Volume 2 of Pepys' diaries, The Master and Fellows of Magdalene College, Cambridge; *cr*: *A View Down a Corridor*, S. van Hoogstraten, National Trust, Photographic Library

Pages 38-39 Dutch specialities
p38: *b*: *The Avenue, Middelharnis*, Meindert Hobbema, NGL **p39:** *tl*: *Interior of St. Bavo's Church, Haarlem*, National Galleries of Scotland, Edinburgh; *tr*: From *Perspective*, Jan Vredeman de Vries, Dover Publications, Inc., New York, 1968; *cr*: Universal surveying instrument designed by Baldassare Lanci, Science Museum, Florence; *b*: *A View of Delft*, Carel Fabritius, NGL

Pages 40-41 Daring illusionism
p40: *Allegory of the Missionary Work of the Jesuits*, Andrea Pozzo, Sant' Ignazio, Rome/thanks to the Rector of S. Ignazio **p41:** *tl*: From Pozzo's *Perspective in Painting and Architecture*, Dover Publications, Inc., New York, 1989; *tr*: Pozzo's Dome, Sant' Ignazio/thanks to the Rector, S. Ignazio; *b*: Perspective Arcade, Francesco Borromini, Palazzo Spada, Rome

Pages 42-43 The magic eye
p42: *tl*: Drawing instrument box, Science Museum, Florence; *tr*: Canaletto's drawings of *The Grand Canal, looking toward Ca'Rezzonico*, Dover Publications, Inc., New York, 1991; *b*: *The Upper Reaches of the Grand Canal with S. Simeone Piccolo*, Canaletto, NGL **p43:** *tl*: Camera obscura, Joshua Reynolds, SM; *tr*: *"The Music Lesson"* – full catalog title, *A Lady at the Virginals with a Gentleman*, Jan Vermeer, Royal Collection, St. James's Palace © Her Majesty The Queen; *c*: Interior of model made for BBC TV program "Take Nobody's Word For It" © Philip Steadman; *c* (bottom): "Take Nobody's Word For It," © BBC; *bl*: Camera obscura, SM

Pages 44-45 Ingenious devices
p44: *tl*: From *Practical Perspective*, Cigoli, Dept. of Prints and Drawings, Uffizi, Florence; *ct*: *"The Mill"* – full catalog title, *Landscape with the Marriage of Isaac and Rebekah*, Claude Lorrain, NGL; *ctr*: Claude Glass, SM; *bl*: Zograscope, SM; *c*: John Farey's Ellipsograph, The British Architectural Library, RIBA, London **p45:** *tl*: James Watt's apparatus, SM; *tc*: Wollaston's Camera Lucida, SM; *tr, cr*: Varley's Graphic Telescope with lens and eyepieces, SM: *cl*: Stereoscopic prints, Bernard Howarth-Loomes; *b*: Wheatstone's Stereoscope, SM; Stereoscopic prints in Wheatstone's Stereoscope: Bernard Howarth-Loomes

Pages 46-47 Dreams of infinity
p46: *tl*: Frontispiece of Sir Isaac Newton's *Mathematical Principles (Principia)*, Vol I, 1729 (Motte translation), BL; *cl*: *The Ancient of Days*, William Blake, BM; *cr*: Engraved plates, nos CCXXXVII and CCXXXVIII by John Farey, from the *Edinburgh Encyclopedia* (1808-30); *b*: The Drawing Academy, Amsterdam, 1764, R. Vinkeles, Victoria & Albert Museum, London **p47:** *tl*: Full title, *Light and Color (Goethe's Theory) – The Morning After the Deluge – Moses Writing the Book of Genesis*, J.M.W. Turner, TG; *tr*: Spheres and frieze from Turner's perspective lectures, TG; *b*: *The Plains of Heaven*, John Martin, TG

Pages 48-49 East meets West
p48: *tl*: Whistler's butterfly signature (detail from *Nocturne in Blue and Green*), TG; *l*: *Nocturne in Blue and Gold: Old Battersea Bridge*, J.A.M. Whistler, TG; *br*: *Kyo-bashi Bridge & Take-gashi*, Ando Hiroshige, from the series of prints, *100 Views of Famous Places in Edo*, BM **p49:** *tl*: *Le Champ de Courses. Jockeys amateurs près d'une voiture (Race Course)*, Edgar Degas, Musée d'Orsay, Paris; *tr*: *Cartwheel by the Seashore*, Ando Hiroshige, from the series *100 Views of Famous Places in Edo*, BM; *cl*: Japanese folding screen, Collection les Indiennes, Paris; *cr*: *Cat Looking at Fields at Asakusa*, Ando Hiroshige, from the series *100 Views of Famous Places in Edo*, BM; *bl*: *Poplars on the Epte*, Claude Monet, TG

Pages 50-51 A personal perspective
p50: *tr*: Max Beckmann, Archiv Fur kunst und Geschicte, Berlin; *bl*: *The Deposition*, by the Master of the St. Bartholomew altarpiece, NGL *cl*: WWI soldier, the Trustees of the Imperial War Museum **p51:** *t*: Still from Robert Wiene's film, *The Cabinet of Dr. Caligari*, British Film Institute, London **pp50-51:** *b*: *Family Picture (Familienbild)*, Max Beckmann, Museum of Modern Art, New York/Artothek

Pages 52-53 New visions of space
p52: *t*: *Mountains in Provence*, Paul Cézanne, NGL; *cr*: Picasso in his villa "La Californie," Cannes, Hulton-Deutsch Collection; *bl*: *Les Demoiselles d'Avignon*, Pablo Picasso, 1906 © DACS 1992, Museum of Modern Art/Giraudon; *br*: African/Bakongo mask, BM/Michael Holford **p53:** *tl*: *Candlestick*, Georges Braque, Scottish National Gallery of Modern Art, Edinburgh; *br*: *Pictorial Architectonic*, Lyubov Popova, Scottish Nat. Gall. Mod. Art, Edinburgh; *bl*: African/Makonde mask, Museum fur Volkerkunde, Munich/Michael Holford

Pages 54-55 Into the future
p54: *tr*: *Le Figaro*, Paris; *l*: *Unique Forms of Continuity in Space*, Umberto Boccioni, TG; *br*: *Victory of Samothrace*, late 3rd-early 2nd century B.C., Louvre, Paris **p55:** *t & br*: *The Street Enters the House*, Umberto Boccioni, Sprengel Museum, Hannover; *bl*: *The Slap*, 1912, Anton Giulio Bragaglia

Pages 56-57 Subtle deception
p56: *br*: *The Disquieting Muses*, Giorgio de Chirico, 1916-17 © DACS 1992, Staatsgalerie Moderner Kunst, Munich **p57:** *cl*: Paul Klee's Studio, © Billdarchiv Felix Klee; *tr*: Das Bauhaus, aus: Berlin Tageblatt, Beilage Weltspiegel, October 1932, Bauhaus-Archiv, Berlin, Atelier Schneider Leihgebührund Leihfrist s. Lieterschein; *cr & b*: *Phantom Perspective*, Paul Klee, 1920, © DACS 1992, The Metropolitan Museum of Art, New York, The Berggruen Klee Collection, 1984 (1984.315.18 / 1984.315.22)

Pages 58-59 Ambiguous space
p58: *tr*: *Domaine d'Arnheim (The Domain of Arnheim)*, René Magritte, Arthur Young, Philadelphia/Artothek © ADAGP, Paris and DACS, London 1992; *cl*: Photograph of Salvador Dali, Dept. Stills, Posters & Designs, British Film Institute, London; *b*: *The Persistence of Memory*, Salvador Dali, Museum of Modern Art, New York/BAL **p59:** *tr*: *Other World* © 1947 M.C. Escher, Cordon Art, Baarn, Holland; *cl*: Plate III, *The Prisons (Le Carceri)*, Giovanni Battista Piranesi, Dover Publications, Inc., New York, 1973; *bl*: Ames's room, John Hedgecoe

Pages 60-61 Popular perspective
p60: *l*: *Just what is it that makes today's homes so different, so appealing?*, 1956, © Richard Hamilton 1992 All rights reserved DACS, Kunsthalle Tübingen, Slg. Zundel, Germany/Artothek; *br*: *The Courtyard of a House in Delft*, Pieter de Hooch, NGL **p61:** *tl*: *Life* Magazine cover: June 1, 1962, The Advertising Archives; *tr*: *Blam*, 1962, © Roy Lichtenstein/DACS 1992, Collection of Richard Brown Baker Courtesy Yale University Art Gallery, New Haven; *bl*: *The Supper at Emmaus*, Caravaggio, NGL; *cr*: "Britons – Kitchener Wants You" WWI poster, Trustees of the Imperial War Museum, London

Page 62 Glossary
Page 62: *tr*: Detail from *The Presentation in the Temple*, Lorenzetti (see p10)

Index

Acknowledgments

Dorling Kindersley would like to thank:

t: top; *b*: bottom; *c*: center; *l*: left; *r*: right

Photography for Dorling Kindersley:
Philip Gatward and his assistant Jeremy Hopley for all their hard work on location photography in Italy (p10: *tr, br, cl*; p14: *cl*; p15: *tc, tl*; p17: *cr*, and back cover *br*; p21: *tr*; p24: *cr & b*; p27: *cl*, and back cover *cr*; pp30-31: all except p31 *tr & br*; pp40-41: all except p41 *tl*; p44: *tl*); Michael Dent (p42: *cr*); Philippe Sebert (p17: *tr*, right-hand panel; p26: *tl*; p54: *br*); and the DK Studio, for additional photography.

For illustrations:
David Cuzik (p12 *c*); Nick Farnell (p43 *br*/this is a copy, made with his permission, of an artwork devised by and copyrighted to Dr. Philip Steadman); Nicholas Hall (p24 *br*); Kuo Kang Chen (pp4, 6, 9 *br*, 12-13 *t*, 13 *cr*, 17 *tr*, 21, 33 and back cover *tl*, 62 *tl*, and artworks for diagrams 1-3, 4, 8). Thanks to Jessica Cole for her drawing (p9 *bl*).

The artwork reconstruction of how the three Uccello paintings may have originally hung (p17 *tr*) is based, with his kind permission, on Dr. Volker Gebhardt's artwork, featured in his article "Some Problems in the Reconstruction of Uccello's *Rout of San Romano* Cycle," published in the *Burlington Magazine*, March

1991. The artwork on p18 (*br*): Reproduced after Marilyn Aronberg Lavin, *Piero della Francesca: The Flagellation*, New York, 1972, FIG.23.

For technical analyses:
Many thanks to Nick Farnell for all the time, hard work, and patience he devoted to devising the technical analyses, with the further advice of Dr. Philip Steadman, on the following pages: p13, p15 *bl & br*, p17 *br*, p21 *cl*, p22 *cr*/cover, p24 *br*, p25 *br*/back cover *c*, p35 *cl*, p38 *tr*, p56 *bl*. Thanks to Claire Pegrum for producing these, and other technical artworks, as computer-generated images (p13 *b*, p15 *bl & br*, p17 *br*, p21 *cl*, p22 *cr*, p25 *cr*/back cover, p35 *cl*, p38 *tr*, p40 *c*, p56 *bl*, p59 *br*, p62: artworks for diagrams 5, 6, and 7).

For all their help in Florence and Rome:
To the Ministero Per i Beni Culturali e Ambientali/Soprintendenza Per i Beni Artistici e Storici delle Provincie di Firenze e Pistoia, for their help and permissions with all location photography in Florence; Signora Palliconi, for her help at the Soprintendenza Per i Beni Artistici e Storici delle Provincie di Firenze e Pistoia; Giulia Di Tommaso for her research help in Florence; Padre Grossi from Santa Maria Novella, Florence, for his valuable help with the Masaccio research; Dr. Dillon, at the Uffizi, Florence; the Ministero dell'Interno,

Direzione Generale degli Affari dei Culti (Direttore: Prefetto Dott. Aldo Camporota) and the Ministero Per i Beni Culturali e Ambientali/Soprintendenza Per i Beni Artistici e Storici di Roma, the Soprintendenza Archeologica di Roma, and the Direttore dell'Accademia Nazionale dei Lincei, for their help and permissions with all location photography in Rome; Dottoressa Todara for her patience at the Ministero dell'Interno, Rome; the staff at the Palatine Archeological Museum, Palatine Hill, Rome.

Many thanks are also due to:
The National Gallery consultants: David Bomford, Jill Dunkerton, Erika Langmuir, and Nicholas Penny, for all their helpful comments; Patricia Williams in the National Gallery Publications Department, and, in the same department, Emma Shackleton for all her hard work; Belinda Ross and Lisa Harris from the National Gallery Reproduction Department, for their patience and efficiency; Darius Wilson, for making models (p17, pp26-27/back cover *cr*/p2); the following for lending objects: Hamleys, London, for the chessboard (pp6-7); Arthur Middleton for the dividers (p4/p18); Gore Booker Interiors, London, for the candlestick, and Jayems, London, for the pipe (p53); Morgans, London, for the vintage television (p60); the photographic departments of The Science Museum, London, The British Museum, London, and the Warburg Institute,

University of London; Jürgen Hinrichs, from Artothek, Germany; Wallace Fox, for the loan of reference material; The Dorling Kindersley Picture Library; Jude Welton, Luisa Caruso, Caroline Juler, and Helen Castle for all their editorial contributions; Hilary Bird, for preparing the index.

A special thanks to Caroline Lucas, for her work on picture research.

Author's acknowledgments
I would like to thank the following people for their help and generosity with this book: the National Gallery team, for all of their helpful comments and opinions; Philip Steadman, for his invaluable advice on perspective matters; the Science Museum, for their advice on optical devices, and Bernard Howarth-Loomes for his patience and time spent advising on stereoscopes; Julia Harris-Voss and Sam Cole for their enthusiastic and energetic research in Rome and Florence; and Ian Chilvers and the Warburg Institute, London University, for the use of their extensive libraries.

Additional thanks are due to Keith Shadwick, for his support and encouragement, and to the following members of the Eyewitness Art team: Sean Moore, Toni Rann, Julia Harris-Voss, and Caroline Lucas; with a special thanks to my editor, Ann Kay, for her sensitivity and thoroughness.

1 BIRD

2 ROCKS & MINERALS

3 SKELETON

4 ARMS & ARMOR

5 TREE

6 POND & RIVER

7 BUTTERFLY & MOTH

8 SPORTS

9 SHELL

10 EARLY HUMANS

11 MAMMAL

12 MUSIC

13 DINOSAUR

14 PLANT

15 SEASHORE

16 FLAG

17 INSECT

18 MONEY

19 FOSSIL

20 FISH

21 CAR

22 FLYING MACHINE

23 ANCIENT EGYPT

24 ANCIENT ROME

25 CRYSTAL & GEM

26 REPTILE

27 INVENTION

28 WEATHER

29 CAT

30 BIBLE LANDS

31 EXPLORER

32 DOG

33 HORSE

34 FILM

35 COSTUME

36 BOAT

37 ANCIENT GREECE

38 VOLCANO & EARTHQUAKE

39 TRAIN

40 SHARK

41 AMPHIBIAN

42 ELEPHANT

43 KNIGHT

44 MUMMY

45 COWBOY

46 WHALE

47 AZTEC, INCA & MAYA

48 BOOK

49 CASTLE

50 VIKING

51 DESERT

52 PREHISTORIC LIFE

53 PYRAMID

54 JUNGLE

55 ANCIENT CHINA